JUSTICE, RECONCILIATION AND PEACE IN AFRICA

DAVID W. SHENK

**INITIALLY TITLED
PEACE & RECONCILIATION IN AFRICA**

FOREWORD Prof John S. Mbiti
APPENDIX Bishop Festo Kivengere

D1158945

UZima

Revised Edition, 1997

ISBN 9966-855-45-9

Published by
Uzima Press
Parliament Road,
Imani House, 2nd Floor
P.O. Box 48127, Nairobi.

Printed by
Act Print Ltd
P.O. Box 48127
Nairobi

**In Memoriam,
the Most Rev. Janani Luwum ...**

'Welcome, Makka. Where have you come from?
With laughter he replied, 'I have come from home!'
'On foot!'
'Yes, of course!'
'Twenty-four miles on foot! Welcome. What brings you to
our home?'
'I have come to ask for forgiveness. Two years ago I became
angry with you. My anger is cleared now. I want to be in peace. I
have come to seek reconciliation.'

a Zanaki Christian.

'They offered me a gun. They wanted me to fight our enemies. I
could not accept the gun. How could I shoot my brother for whom
Christ shed his blood.'

a Gikuyu Christian.

CONTENTS

FOREWORD

Dr. Shenk's book, *Justice, Reconciliation and Peace* addresses itself to an extremely important concern. The theme is as old as the human race itself. Wherever people are found, whether in Africa or elsewhere, the sinful elements of strife, conflict, tension, dissention and war surface in one form or another. Justice, Reconciliation and peace are necessary in order to overcome these destroyers of human society.

It is both relevant and urgent, to examine the way in which the African people have struggled to cultivate peace and reconciliation in their traditional life as well as in the midst of their contemporary experiences. Even though the words 'peace and reconciliation' are strictly religious terms, the secular and the religious worlds use them and need them equally. In this book, however, Dr. Shenk concentrates on the more religious dimensions of these terms. He draws from the African Religion and Christianity in Africa, since the latter is spreading rapidly in the southern two thirds of Africa (including Malagasy) where the African Religion has predominated previously. We cannot look at major religious themes in this region of Africa without taking into consideration these two religious traditions.

To achieve the above aim, Dr. Shenk briefly introduces aspects of African Religion to provide the background (for the reader who may not be so familiar with it), to his discussion. The author assumes, and perhaps wrongly in some cases, that the reader will have a working knowledge of how Christianity came to Africa in the early centuries of the Church as well as in more recent times. He rightly observes that God 'desires peace' and that He is 'pre-eminently concerned about justice, reconciliation and peace among people'. This theological insight is present in both the African Religion and Christianity. When these two religious views meet, they dovetail without overt conflict. One affirms the other, and one strengthens the other.

The presentation of the book is seasoned with interesting illustrations and examples of peace and reconciliation from many parts of Africa. Dr. Shenk draws heavily from his own experience of having been born in Tanzania, of having missionary parents, and of later working in Kenya. This is a great advantage since he has participatory and intimate knowledge of the African society. At the same time, as an American missionary, he can also look at Africa from a distance and with objectivity. He selects and discusses issues not only as academic areas of exploration, but also as living realities. The all-embracing nature of his subject matter would make it impossible to study in depth how justice, reconciliation and peace relate to all areas of society. So he draws our attention to select issues such as marriage covenant, the brutalities of some military regimes, the demonic forces during the era of apartheid in South Africa, the East African Revival movement, and so on. In some cases the struggling people find justice, reconciliation and peace; in other cases they hope for them but die without ever experiencing real peace.

The book is highly readable, well documented and informative. No book can cover everything under the sun. But I wish that *Justice, Reconciliation and Peace* would have treated more seriously apartheid era in southern Africa. The demonic system of apartheid challenged us all to the very depths of our concern for justice, reconciliation and peace. It was a system of violence through its oppression and exploitation of African peoples by the immigrant minority from Europe. Apartheid was a blatant violation of human rights and a satanic denial of the Gospel of our Lord Jesus Christ. Many people in southern Africa sought for justice, reconciliation and peace. Some of them were driven to the point of desperation. Some lifted the gun, others opened the Bible—and all in search of peace, justice and the distribution of power (political, economic, educational and ecclesiastical).

In the book I also miss two other important considerations. One is peace and reconciliation between the human race and the world of nature on the one hand—the land, the environment and the animal kingdom—and the world of technology on the other. The other is a discussion of the personal dimension of peace, the peace which comes out of a reconciled spirit and mind. This is the kind of peace about which St. Paul wrote, that 'the peace of God which passes all understanding, will keep your hearts and your minds in Christ Jesus' (Phil. 4: 7).

I am grateful to my friend for asking me to write this short foreword to his book. I am even more grateful that he has taken the time and done the research, in order to write down in a consistent way, these reflections on justice, reconciliation and peace. They are universal concerns and I hope that many people will benefit as I have from reading this book. I am writing these words at Advent time, and so I feel very conscious of the Christian message of Advent—a message of peace and reconciliation. Dr. Shenk's book is an appropriate reminder that his message is for all times and all seasons, as much in Africa as in the rest of the world .

John Mbiti

ACKNOWLEDGEMENTS

Most of what I have written has been absorbed through a lifetime of living and working in East Africa. I acknowledge my debt to that African community of humankind through whom I have been nurtured. From 1973 to 1979 I was a lecturer in the Department of Philosophy and Religious Studies at Kenyatta University college in Kenya. I taught Christianity in Africa, Comparative Religion, and Religion as a Phenomenon. That experience of intense academic interchange with Kenyan university students was a great joy. The process of classroom interaction helped to sharpen my vision. Their term papers and research projects increased appreciation of African insights which I had hitherto absorbed only unconsciously. I am most grateful to my students and university colleagues for sharing freely of their experiences and heritage.

For documentation I have drawn from the great store of archival treasures which are available at Kenyatta University College, whose value cannot be exaggerated. These research documents by university students are prime evidence of a heritage which is vanishing. They record a multitude of interviews with sages who remember a time when there was no church in their land. These wise men and women are old people now. Within a few more years their memory will be lost forever. What these students have recorded now, while the memory of a dying generation is still tractable, is becoming the principal window into the past. Without that window I could never have recorded some of the reflections which this book contains. I am grateful to the university for the privilege of looking through that window into the past by reading the dissertations, theses and research papers which are kept in the research archives.

I also acknowledge the kindness of the Eastern Mennonite Board of Missions and Charities, Salunga, Pennsylvania who graciously provided me with a one-year sabbatical for research and writing. They also provided an office and secretarial help.

I am also deeply grateful to friends and scholars who have read and evaluated the manuscript. Their comments have been exceedingly helpful. I think, especially, of the following: the Rev.

Ronald Dain, formerly chairman of the Department of Philosophy and Religious Studies, Kenyatta University College; the Rt. Rev. Horace Etemesi, formerly Managing Editor, Uzima Press, Nairobi; Dr. Donald R. Jacobs, secretary, Overseas Ministries, Eastern Mennonite Board of Missions and Charities: Mr. Stephen Kamau, associate director, Department of Research and Theological Development, National Christian Council of Kenya; Rt. Rev. Zedekiah Kisare, bishop, Tanzania Mennonite Church; Mr. Jonathan Kariara, Nairobi, Kenya; Mrs. Rosalyn Kniss, co-directoress, Eastleigh Fellowship Centre, Nairobi; Prof. John S. Mbiti, director, The Ecumenical Institute, Geneva; Mr. Harold Miller, development officer, National Christian Council of Kenya; Mr. Jesse N.K. Mugambi, lecturer, Department of Philosophy and Religious Studies, University of Nairobi; the late Rev. Heshbon Mwangi, formerly pastor, Kahuhia Parish, Church of the Province of Kenya; Rev. Scotch Ndlovu, seminarian, Associate Mennonite Biblical Seminaries, Elkhart, Indiana; Dr. Zablon Nthamburi, Presiding Bishop of the Methodist Church in Kenya and former lecturer, Department of Philosophy and Religious Studies, Kenyatta University College; the Rev. Joshua Okello, evangelist, Kenya Mennonite Church; the Rev. J. Clyde Shenk, former pastor, Kenya Mennonite Church; the Rev. Joseph Shenk, co-ordinator Mennonite Board in Eastern Africa; Dr. Norman E. Thomas, School of Theology, Boston University; the Rev. David Trollope, director, CORAT, Nairobi; Dr. B.K. Wambari, chairman, Department of Philosophy and Religious Studies, Kenyatta University College; the Rev. & Mrs. Ron Ward, missionaries, African Christian Church and Schools, Kenya; Mrs Ruth Zimmerman and Miss Linda Nafziger who made additions and corrections to the original manuscript, and to Grace, my dear wife, who with our four children, was an inspiration to me throughout this writing effort, who through encouragement kept me constantly on track and did all the manuscript typing.

INTRODUCTION

I believe that the African quest for the harmony of man in community is really a quest for 'peace'. That is what this book is about: Justice, *Reconciliation and Peace in Africa*. Mine is an interpretation of some aspects of African Christian experience in the quest for justice, reconciliation and peace. It is an attempt to probe justice and reconciliation themes in Africa's pre-christian heritage first, and then describe and interpret the Gospel of Peace as it is experienced and expressed by many Christians in Africa today. The book is written with the conviction that many of the churches in modern Africa today have joyously recaptured aspects of apostolic faith and life whose experience can be a blessing to all of us.

The books on traditional African religion occupy a wide swath of my professional book-shelf. Most have been written within the past two decades. Probably Professor John S. Mbiti has been the pace-setter with a cluster of titles written within the past fifteen years. I hope African scholars will continue the excellent research and writing which has characterized the past several decades of African theological and religious publication. This book is not an attempt to recapitulate or further elaborate the insights which African scholarship is developing in this last half of the twentieth century. The intent of this study is narrow in scope; it is focused on reconciliation motifs within the African experience, with the aim of deepening the reader's understanding of African approaches to reconciliation from both a traditional and a Christian Atrican viewpoint.

The reflections which follow are particularly related to my experiences in East Africa; Tanzania, where I was born and raised, and Somalia and Kenya, where I have lived and worked as an adult. Yet this book is not limited to the East African experience only. Illustrative material is included from a wide spectrum of sub-Saharan societies, and many of the observations are just as relevant to the general sub-Saharan panorama as to East Africa specifically.

This book is a celebration of joy for me, the celebration of childhood roots and adult relationships, East Africa is my home.

My parents were pioneer missionaries among the Zanaki in the Tanzanian hilly lands twenty miles east of Lake Victoria. All of my best boyhood friends were Tanzanians. We played and fought together. Many of my deepest values were absorbed in these early relationships. I came to learn that African values are people centered: Relationships are the essence of life. A person can only be person in community. These are indigenous African insights, which I value deeply.

I am thankful for the values which Africans have taught me. Perhaps my appreciation has to some extent obscured my objectivity. I see so much that is good in the traditional heritage, that I probably fail to observe with appropriate balance that which is not ideal. So be it. It is not my intention to judge nor search for deficiencies in the cultures or traditions of others. I have consciously determined to absorb the good with thankfulness, to think on. 'whatever is just, whatever is pure, whatever is gracious . . .' (Philippians 4: 8). It is the good which enriches, and I have attempted to describe some of the good in the African heritage which has been a help to me.

One of the greatest joys of my adult life has been the experience of participating in the 'Christianization' of traditional African values. I grew up in an African community which was hearing the Gospel for the first time. As an adult I have lived in an Africa which has already embraced the Gospel, and where in the process the human insight of the African heritage have been tremendously enriched, affirmed, expanded, and to some extent revolutionized.

The enrichment of African human values through the Gospel is one side of the story. A more sombre reality is that the tidal wave of western culture on which the Gospel rode into Africa has often undermined the humane underpinnings of traditional values. *Things* are replacing *relationships* as the measuring stick of progress. Wealth rather than quality of life through meaningful relationships is becoming the criteria of success. The gross national product is becoming the touchstone of development aspirations. These forms of westernization are neither Christian nor African. Individualistic materialism is a tragic perversion of the African heritage.

Yet across the continent of Africa there are communities of Christian faith who have not betrayed their birthright for a transient pot of porridge. Relationships are the essence of their Christian faith and experience. They live the Gospel in relationships. Injustice, family and community tensions, and even international issues are processed within the redemptive framework of the Church, the new community in which the love of God has tremendously enriched the traditional African experience of the person in community.

I believe that the redemption of the person in community is the soul of authentic African perceptions of the Gospel. It is not surprising that many western interpretations of the Gospel seem superficial to many who have been nurtured within the soul of African Christian faith. The western theologian asks: What is the right doctrine? The African Church asks: What are the right relationships? In the west, good Christianity is good doctrine. In Africa reconciliation and power are the touchstone of faith. Although these contrasts are oversimplified generalizations, anyone who has lived in both worlds recognizes that Christ as Lord is usually interpreted quite differently in the two contexts.

As we listen to these different interpretations our faith will be mutually enriched. Usually it is the African Church which receives the 'blessing' of being enriched by the faith experience of the western Church. The enrichment has flowed mostly in one direction. This book is an attempt to help reverse the flow. Already a cluster of African Christian writers have begun the process of interpreting their faith experience to the larger community of humankind; President Dr. Julius Nyerere, President Dr. Kenneth Kaunda, Prof. John S. Mbiti, President Prof. Leopold Senghor, Prof. John S. Bobee, Rt. Rev. Festo Kivengere, to mention only a few. This book is an attempt to contribute to this growing body of African Christian literature.

I write as a debtor. I am not an African, but I have been blessed through participation in the life of the Church in Africa. I desire to share that experience as it has affected me in the hope that others can be similarly blessed. In a sense, this book is a personal testimonial.

My testimonial, my particular perceptions of Christian faith have also been affected by my Mennonite Anabaptist heritage. The Mennonite Church is my denominational home. The Menonites are the spiritual descendents of the Anabaptists of sixteenth century in Europe, who believed that man is saved in community. For them the essence of the Church was the fact that two or three met in fellowship in the name of Jesus. It is the meeting in his name which is the Church, not necessarily whether the word is rightly preached, or the priest rightly ordained, or the eucharist rightly shared. For the Anabaptists it was the *fellowship* of believers which was the Church. The Anabaptists believed that the fellowship of believers was a reconciling community, an experience and expression of peace.

I believe my Anabaptist Mennonite Christian heritage has helped me to notice and appreciate certain African perceptions of salvation, justice, reconciliation, and peace in community which I would have otherwise overlooked. My own background leads me to affirm with profound appreciation forms of African Christian expression which are also fellowship-centred. In fact, my involvement with the Church in Africa has deepened my appreciation for my Anabaptist roots. Especially in East Africa, where spiritual renewal has been accompanied by a profound commitment to fellowship, justice, reconciliation and peace, in other words salvation in community, I have rediscovered my own spiritual heritage.

I have written from the perspective of one who is committed to Jesus Christ and Biblical faith. I believe the Gospel of Christ is the fulfilment of the quest for peace which all peoples ultimately seek.

This book is a reflection on a pilgrimage of discovery. Some will not agree with the nature of the discovery. Some may even suggest that I have discovered aspects of Christian experience in Africa which are hardly present. Admittedly all pilgrimages in faith affirmation and discovery are ultimately intensely personal and subjective. Yet the pearl of personal discovery should not be hidden; in the disclosure of the pearl others are often also blessed. That is the intention of this book.

PART ONE

Traditional African Experience
of Justice, Reconciliation and Peace.

Thaai!
Thathaiya Ngai,
Thai !

Peace We beseech thee God,
Peace ! — A *Gikuyu Prayer*

Chapter I

THE BLESSING OF PEACE IN COMMUNITY

It is so much fun meeting friends. The embraces. The rolling laughter. The joyful sharing of news. Invariably the feasting. I always feel cleansed after such reunions. Reunion after separation is a celebration event. It is the reaffirmation of a community.

Farewells are the same. Feasting to celebrate the good times people have had together. Laudatory accounts of the good will which has bound friends together. The prayers of blessing. The sharing of gifts which will help cement the relationship, amidst the separation.

African societies everywhere idealize the community. They also have clear vision of the spiritual dynamics of the ideal society. This chapter is an attempt to describe that ideal. I suppose that no African society has ever fully lived the ideal. Yet the shape of the good community is quite clearly understood. What follows is a description of aspects of that commonly perceived good.

God, The Creator of Life and Peace

African peoples have always believed in God the creator. Wherever the Bible is translated into African languages, the indigenous term for God is used. The belief in God the creator is not debatable.

However, there is ambiguity concerning the nature of God. Is he a personal or an impersonal life force? Is he transcendent or pantheistic? Is he theistic or deistic, presently involved in creation or uninvolved? These questions hover over traditional concepts of God in hazy ambiguity. African scholars themselves are divided on what the authentic African perception of God has been. For example, Dr. Samuel Kibicho believes that the Gikuyu of Kenya have always been theistic, but Dr. Alexis Kagame of Rwanda interprets divinity in Africa almost pantheistically. Both may be right. Variety is the genius of African religiosity.

Although each African society has its distinctiveness, we now know that there is also sufficient commonalty within the wide range

3

of inter African traditional beliefs to allow specific case studies to be made and to apply insights gained in this manner to the wider dimensions of Africa's traditional religious experience. In this chapter we shall specifically describe the concepts of God among the traditional Gikuyu of Kenya.

Intelligent discussion of traditional concepts is complicated by the rapid Christianization and Islamization of Africa during the past century. Original concepts have been extensively coloured by the pervasive monotheism of Christian and Islamic expansion. Nevertheless, when one reads the literature available, including documents from the earliest missionary encounter with sub-Saharan Africa, the impression is that Africans as a whole have always been theistically inclined. This is certainly the conclusion of missionary scholars such as the Methodist Edwin Smith or the Catholic Placide Tempels.[2] Both, writing from the perspective of the first half of this century, accepted that the God whom Africans know is similar in many respects to the God whom Christians worship. Recent African scholarship further affirms those earlier missionary insights. Bishop Tempels was probably not far wrong in pointing out that God is the Great Person, the One from whom all life and power flows, and the One to whom we progressively return as we move through the prescribed stages in life.

Rather than survey the abundance of contemporary writings concerning the African perceptions of God, I shall focus on Dr. Samuel Kibicho's doctoral research on the traditional Gikuyu concepts of God.[3] Although we cannot determine to what extent Kibicho's study has been infiltrated by Christian perceptions, it is my impression that his insights must be taken seriously. One reason for accepting Kibicho's theistic hypothesis is that a number of outstanding African scholars are in general agreement with him, as for example the writings of Prof. John S. Mbiti from East Africa or Prof. E. Bolaji Idowu of West Africa.

Idowu, writing from a West African perspective, has described the traditional Yoruba perceptions of God in his case study, *Olodumare, God in Yoruba Belief.*[4] On the other hand Mbiti's *Concepts of God in Africa*[5] *is* a panoramic survey of God belief in a wide variety of African societies. Both Mbiti's general survey and Idowu's more particular investigation reveal that at least a latent theism is pervasive in sub-Saharan Africa; in some societies the theistic impulse dominates the religious experience of the people. This seems, for example, to be the case among the Nuer of the Sudan.[6] Theism was also the unifying motif of Gikuyu traditional religion, their perceptions of the moral and righteous character of God contributed significantly and positively to the struggle for independence in Kenya.

The Gikuyu have always believed that God is the Life Giver. He is pre-eminently revealed through the gift of human life, and his greatest desire for people is the 'enhancement of life in the community'.[7] Life is God's greatest gift. Life is 'the greatest sign of his benevolent presence and power'.[8] God not only gives life; he also sustains it. The earth and the rain are his gifts to nourish life. That which contributes to life is sacred because it is a gift from God. The earth is especially sacred for it is through the earth that all forms of life become possible. All the aspects of human existence which sustain and nourish life are sacred gifts from God, the Life-Giver.[9]

God's life-giving gifts are abundant. For example, He gives to each people their inheritance of land. In fact, among the Gikuyu, God is often referred to as the 'Divider of Land'. The land of a people is the people's inheritance from God for the sustenance of life. To seize the land of another is to steal the source of life which God has given. Land stealing is a crime against God, against life, against humanity. This precious, life-sustaining gift from God could not be sold among many societies. It is for this reason that, among the Gikuyu, land could never be sold commercially to an outsider, and European immigration and colonial expansionism made no sense in Gikuyu theological perceptions. Missionaries were often asked by the Gikuyu whether God had not given their peoples (the white tribes) land or cattle in the country from which they had come.

It was theologically perplexing that the Divider of the Land had not given consideration to the white people when he divided out the lands of the earth. It was inconceivable that a people who had received land from God would try to seize the land of another people. To seize land was to strangle life; it was an act against divine order and harmony.[10]

Land is a tangible gift from God. There are also intangible life sustaining gifts. For example, God provides the community with the personal talents necessary for harmonious relationships. Some people are especially wise; they are the counsellors. Other people are fools; they provide humour. Others are blacksmiths; they provide the implements for farming. Others are especially gifted as farmers. These multiple talents are life-nourishing gifts from God. They help to sustain the community of man.[11]

God as the Life giver and Divider of Land is also the God of peace and justice. In fact, in Gikuyu traditional theology God is pre-eminently the God of justice. His justice is revealed in the human community. Kibicho writes, 'the one true God for the Gikuyu, and for the African people generally, is and always has been above everything else, the God of socio-political justice'.[12] Africans have an amazing confidence in God as the Just One. Whenever injustice seems to prevail, the Swahili say *Mungu yuko* (God is present). The implication is, be patient and persistent; God will eventually bring justice to pass. Similarly when two people have a disagreement, the argument can be readily dismissed by saying, 'God will judge between us'. When our house was robbed, many of our African friends said, 'Don't worry, God will replace what has been stolen!' Anxiety is unnecessary because God is reliable and he is just.

Complete confidence in God's justice gives African peoples astonishing resiliency. They know that injustice will never ultimately triumph. Therefore stubborn patience and persistence is possible because of the sure hope of eventual justice. At the same time Africans refuse to settle for anything less than justice. To accept indefinite structural injustice would be a negation of God's pre-eminent concern for justice. Kibicho says of the Gikuyu whose lands were confiscated by the colonial powers: 'His faith that God is the God of justice above all else gave him courage to hope against hope that one day he would surely be free'.[13] It was his complete confidence in the justice of God which gave him courage to resist colonialism with determination and to endure enormous hardships in the struggle for independence.

Kibicho points out that truth and wisdom are interwoven with justice. The God of justice is also the God of truth and its corollary, wisdom. Wisdom and truth are inseparable, and both establish justice. In this context some alien forms of justice are incomprehensible. In modern courts a lawyer will argue the innocence of his client even though he knows that his client is guilty. He will represent untruth in a court of justice! In traditional society no respected African elder would ever have done that! The traditional African courts of justice were for the sake of determining the truth so that justice could prevail.[14]

Because God is sovereign, there was absolute confidence that truth and justice would triumph. Kibicho points out that the Gikuyu term for justice is *kihoto* which means truth, reason, or right judgement. Interestingly the Gikuyu term, *hota,* means 'be able', 'be capable'. 'win', or 'be victorious'. Justice wins! God cannot be defeated.[15]

God also establishes peace. Wisdom and truth affirm justice. Similarly justice affirms peace. The God of justice is also pre-eminently the God of peace. One of the widely used names for God among the Bantu of East and South Central Africa is *Mulungu* or variations of that name. *Mulungu* suggests power, mercy and goodness.[16] Justice is not a cold reality. It is touched with mercy. It is basically concerned with peace. This is the theme of an ancient Gikuyu prayer, *Thaai, Thathaiya Ngai, Thai,* (Peace, we beseech thee, God, peace). This prayer was offered with hands outstretched facing Mount Kenya from whence God had originally given the Gikuyu people their inheritance among the peoples of the earth. God is the One who desires peace for his people.

People could only approach God in a condition of peace. The great sacrificial festival among the Gikuyu was called the day of peace. Because God desires peace, all forms of interpersonal malevolence had to be cleansed before the people were free to come before God with their petitions. The community had to collectively deal with evil; God could not bless those who compacted with disharmony. God desires peace and, because he is sovereign, peace must prevail.

Although God is the source of all power, most African societies do not blame God for evil. This is because all forms of dehumanization are alien to God. Evil flows from bitterness, envy, malice, and hatred. Evil is attitudinal in origin. Evil is a rejection of peace, an affirmation of disharmony, an anti-person or anti-community spirit. Therefore God, who is the source of life, justice and peace, cannot be blamed for evil.[17] It is for this reason that the Gikuyu never faulted God for the tragic seizure of their lands by the white colonialists. They knew that this injustice and evil could not continue forever. A time would come when the Gikuyu people would unite and rid the land and the community of the malevolence which was destroying life. The victory of justice and peace was certain because of the sovereignty of the Life-Giver.[18]

It is uncertain to what extent the Kibicho study of the Gikuyu traditional perceptions of God as the one who establishes peace and justice can be universalized throughout the African experience. Present research is still too scanty to make generalized judgements. Nevertheless Mbiti affirms that he is not aware of any African society which believes that God is evil,[19] although a few societies seem to attribute no moral principles to God, as for example the Azande of Sudan. Yet the Azande perception seems to be the exception.[20] Evans-Pritchard, who did an exhaustive study of the Nuer in Sudan, has found that God is very much concerned about reconciliation and peace among people. The violation of personhood is profoundly offensive to God. Community disharmony is a violation of the will of God. The Nuer religion is therefore most preoccupied with the establishment of harmony among people; reconciliation and peace constitute good religion and are akin to godliness.[21]

This Nuer prayer reveals the deep spirituality of the person in community: 'Our Father, it is thy universe, it is thy will, let us be at peace, let the souls of the people be cool; thou art our Father, remove all evil from our path.'[22]

Similar themes of justice, peace, and reconciliation emerge in a multitude of other African societies. The Meru of Kenya tell of their founding ancestor, Mugwe, who led his people under the command of God from a country where they had been unjustly enslaved into the land which the Meru now occupy. God is known to the Meru by his acts of justice on their behalf; in a manner which seems to be an echo of the Biblical deliverance of Israel from slavery, God led them to freedom and peace. Even today the heads of the Meru clans are called *Agwe* (sing. *Mugwe*) in memory of the leader who first delivered them from injustice. The *Agwe* today are expected to be men of absolute justice, integrity, and peace for they are the link between God, the Deliverer, and society as a whole.[23]

In West Africa, Professor Bolaji Idowu describes similar beliefs among the Yoruba of Nigeria among whom God is the nodal point of peace, social justice, and harmony. Reconciliatory processes are God-sanctioned. He is the one through whom peace and interpersonal harmony are affirmed, sustained, and nourished.[24]

It is futile to attempt to determine how much Christian or Islamic hangover or theological interpenetration these African perceptions of God and community suggest. I am personally overwhelmed with the pervasive awareness of the presence of God among African Christians. Prayer and awareness of God are constantly at the forefront of all of life. At the same time many Africans themselves have often told me that violations of brotherhood are sins against God. Forgiveness and reconciliation among people are godly; anger and bitterness are sins against God. These are deep convictions and they permeate contemporary African Christianity. These convictions are Biblical, but I believe that these Biblical insights are practised enthusiastically by African Christians because a multitude of them have received from their traditional heritage an inner wellspring of belief in God as the One who pre-eminently affirms and sustains the person in authentic, harmonious community. The Gospel seems to deepen and fulfil insights which have been nourished in the traditional heritage for millenia.

Concepts of God such as 'Divider of the Land', 'Life-Giver', 'Justice', 'Truth', 'Wisdom', and 'Peace', are encompassed in the common Bantu reference to God as the Great *Muntu* (Great Person).[25] He is the nodal point of all existence. All life proceeds from God.

People are personalized differentiations of the great cosmic personal interaction in community which proceeds from God and is sustained and nurtured by him.[26] In other words we cannot speak of God in African terms without at the same time referring to personhood in community. We turn now more explicitly to the African concept of the person in fellowship.

The person in Harmonious Community

The sharing of food together is a profound experience in community. This was especially so in traditional African homes. Some of the traditional symbols are disappearing, but others emerge to perpetuate the symbols of community in eating.

All the participants in the meal wash their hands before and after eating. The act of hand washing is hygienic, to be sure, but it is also a sign of cleansing in preparation for the communion of eating together. Usually a young girl will bring the water pot and she may kneel or curtsy before each person in turn as she offers the gift of water poured out for cleansing. She may have carried that water many miles from the nearest spring—it is a costly gift. The washing of the hands is symbolic of spiritual cleansing needed in order to fully experience the blessing of eating together. Cleansing and communion, servanthood and blessing, are symbolically intertwined in eating together.

In many African societies, all eat from a common dish. Hands reach forward into one dish to partake of the food together. In some societies the elder of the homestead must partake of the food first, as a sign that the food is acceptable and blessed. Then the younger can begin to eat. Often the elder patriarch will take a choice morsel of meat from the common dish, and divide it out among those sharing in the meal. This is a sign of patriarchal blessing and sharing. Life proceeds from the elder to the younger. The elder shares the choicest meat with those who are gathered around his table.

If a stranger passes by, he must be compelled to share in the meal. A stranger is a sign of special blessing. He cannot merely give a greeting and then go on his way. He must join in the meal. He must share in the communal mysticism of the meal. A refusal to share in

10

the meal is the sign of a curse, a negation of communion, a refusal to confirm communal harmony. He must eat. The presence of the stranger is a sign that the communion of the feast has extended beyond the narrow bounds of the immediate family; the wider community of humanity has also symbolically shared in the feast, and the eating has therefore been a special blessing.

The first servings of the meal are for the men. By eating the food which has been prepared by the womenfolk, the men both confirm that the effort of the women was acceptable and symbolically bless those who have prepared it. Similarly, the ones who have prepared the food will pray that the food will bless those who eat it. There is a mystery in eating. Sometimes food can cause illness. The prayers before eating are a recognition that forms of malevolence can linger about the eating experience which could cause illness. The prayers usually include petitions such as "and if there be anything evil, take it away, before we partake of the food". Thus the womenfolk pray that the experience of eating will be blessed, and similarly the men who eat the food thereby accept and bless the effort of the women-folk. So after the men have eaten, the women of the homestead will share the remainder of the food together with the children. All have now eaten. All have communed. All have been blessed. The meal is concluded with a second washing of the hands, an affirmation of cleansing and blessing, a seal on the communion of eating.

This is a brief description of the communion of eating together as I have personally experienced it hundreds of times. Eating is a sacrament of the person in community. It is sign of life-giving harmony. The rhythm of the daily homestead meal is a sign of the rhythm of life and the experience of community. We shall now look in greater depth at the meaning of the person in community as symbolized in eating together.

African religion is anthropocentric. Man is the measure of the good. He is at 'the centre'.[27] Although Kenneth Kaunda, the first president of Zambia, speaks as a modern African Christian intellectual, his interpretation of African humanism is rooted in the traditional insights concerning the centrality of the person in the mind of God and the social order. Both Christian and non-Christian Africans who

11

are informed by their traditional heritage would affirm Dr. Kaunda's declaration:

> Central to my understanding of humanism is the striving towards an ideal of individual fulfilment. I want every member of our society to be given the chance to achieve the best that is in him or her. That is not just a pious cliche; it has vital social and political implications.[28]

This is precisely the position that was developed by other leading African political philosophers and founding fathers of independent nations such as Leopold Senghor of Senegal or Julius Nyerere of Tanzania. The well-being of the person is the criterion for the good. The person is of ultimate significance. In African belief and practice the person is sacred and signficant. The two examples below illustrate it:

> I was five hundred kilometers from home. The road home was good. The drive should take only six hours. As I was preparing to leave, my African bishop called me in for counsel. He commanded that I go with a colleague, even though my friend had no reason for the journey, and would need to return by bus the following day. I insisted that the courtesy was not necessary. But my bishop and his fellow churchmen were insistent, because they said, 'You will be lonely riding alone. A car cannot talk. It is only metal. You need a person to be with you.'
>
> Grandma Mirengeri approached her American pastor, 'We are praying that God will bless your home with more children'.
>
> 'Oh, thank you! But we already have four children. That is sufficient.'
>
> 'How can you say that four children is sufficient blessing? Surely God will bless a man like you with many more children.'
>
> 'But in my country, America, even four children are too many. You see, it is too expensive to have many children.'
>
> 'No. You are wrong,' replied Grandma Mirengeri firmly. 'In your country the streets are filled with cars, but they are empty of

children. In our country the streets are empty of cars, but they are filled with children. Cars are only iron. They have no life. You cannot have fellowship with a car. Therefore, you must know that your country, America, is poor. It is suffering from a great disease. It is more concerned about cars than people. You have stopped having children so that you can have things instead of people. But we are rich in Tanzania. We are blessed with children. And children are eternal.'

Grandmother Mirengeri's comments are an affirmation of the Twi proverb, 'It is man who counts; I call upon gold, it answers not; I call upon drapery, it answers not: It is man who counts.'[29]

In the traditional African experience, work was ideally a celebration of personhood. I recall seeing a film of the traditional African method of smelting iron. As the ore grew hotter and hotter and the bellows were pumped faster and faster, the pumping of the bellows became a dance and a song. Louder and louder the song became, and the dance more and more joyous. When the film ended, my African seat-mate leaned over and said, 'That is the way my grandfather used to work when he was young. Work was celebration; it included song and dance. But now we are modernized. Work isn't celebration any more.'

My colleague was only partly right. For many Africans the celebration of personhood is preserved in the arena of modern work. Laughter and talk are intertwined with work in many Nairobi factories. Even in the office, one often notices people who carry the joy of spontaneity of celebration of life and personhood right into the office routine.

Personhood is affirmed by handshaking. When a guest arrives in a home, he shakes hands with everyone in the house, including the tiny baby. Even in the midst of conversation, when a point is mutually emphasized by two friends, they may spontaneously shake hands. And in farewell, handshaking is performed several times: when you arise to go, perhaps again as you leave the door, and possibly even farther up the street. Through touch the person is affirmed. There is joy in feeling the other person and sensing through his handshake that you also are recognized. All participate in this affirmation experience; even the smallest child is included.

Respect for personhood is also revealed in African attitudes towards sports, and especially wrestling. Idowu mentions the horror he experienced when first seeing American wrestling and boxing. It was for him, and most Africans, incomprehensible that a sport would do bodily harm. Life is sacred. The person is sacred. Bodily harm to the person in the traditional milieu was reprehensible. For instance, among the Yoruba wrestling is a test of strength which avoids any bodily harm. It is done with grace and dignity. When even so much as a finger of an opponent touches the ground, the winner is declared. Oppressing the opponent by sitting on him, or punching him, or wounding him by striking him is not acceptable, because the person is respected.[30]

The dignity of the person is affirmed through the practice of naming children. When a mother senses that she is pregnant there is joy for it is known that a person has been conceived. Abortion is unthinkable. She wonders who the new person will be. As the little person begins to move in the womb, she begins to sense mysteriously the qualities of personhood within her. On rare occasions she may decide the name of the child before it is born, but almost universally the parents will wait until the child has arrived before naming the new person. Sometimes it may take several days or even weeks before the name is decided, because they cannot name the child without knowing who the newborn person is. The child's name is the seal of his personhood. In many societies this seal of personhood is officially given in a special ritual ceremony, when the child receives the inner name, the true name of the person.[31]

As the child progresses through the stages of life, his personal roles will change. New names will be adopted to fit these different roles. But the inner name of the person will remain for ever. The role names are functional and descriptive of work or responsibility. But the inner name is perpetual witness that the person is not his work or his role. The person is more deeply perceived than the chores which he performs.[32]

14

Death ceremonies are also an affirmation of the person. Once I drove a corpse three hundred kilometers to its place of burial Although there was hardly room in my car for an additional person, the relatives appropriately insisted that a brother had to travel with the corpse in my car. To do otherwise would be disrespectful to the person who had departed. After delivering the corpse to the family homestead, I bade farewell to the family members, and began the trip home alone. I had not gone more than five kilometers when my car went into a frightful skid. Although I was able to avoid the potential accident, it seemed to me that the skid had an eeriness about it, for the road surface and driving conditions didn't seem particularly conducive to such a near catastrophe. Later I told some African friends of my near accident.

My friends' immediate question was, 'Did you stay for the funeral?'

'No,' I replied, 'I simply had to get back home that night. I could not wait, but I bade the whole family proper farewell and I prayed with them before departing.'

'But you did not stay for the burial. That is why your car had the skid. You didn't show proper respect for the departed, and he was unhappy. He travelled with you for a while.'

Death is the momentous event in which the person departs from the community of the living and joins the community of the living dead. Death is departure.[33] In the Swahili language, the death of a person is referred to as *fariki* (depart or travel on). *Kufa* (die) is applied to animals. Sometimes *Kufa* is also applied to a dead person in a rather cavalier spirit; *fariki* is never used for a dead animal. It would be beyond the scope of this study to investigate the deeper philosophical and theological meaning of this differentiation. Both Alex Kagame and Janheinz Jahn have explored the concept of personhood in Bantu perceptions of death. In summary, they point out that *Muntu (Muntu:* person; *Bantu:* Persons) is used for the living dead and the living. Both are persons.

The living persons *(Bantu)* who possess biological life are called the *bazima*. The living dead persons *(Bantu)* are called *bazimu*. The participation or non-participation in biological life does not affect

15

the reality of authentic personhood. Both the living and the dead are *Bantu*. Death is the point of transition of the person *(Muntu)* from the state of *bazima* to the condition of *bazimu*. And whether living or living dead, the person *(muntu)* is respected.[34] In *Bantu* cosmology the cause of my near accident was that I had not given sufficient respect to the departed person, although indeed I had paid my appropriate respects to the living.

Respect for the person includes a profound appreciation for personal integrity. Although truth and transparency are valued, nosiness into the affairs of another person is reprehensible. A Baluba proverb says, '*Munda mwa mukwenu kemwelwa kuboko, nansya ulele nandi butanda bumo!*' (None may put his arm into his neighbour's inside, not even when he shares his bed).[35] The conscience of a person is personal and no one, not even his sleeping companion, has the right to probe the inner recesses of his neighbour's spirit.

Although transparency and confession are exceedingly prominent in most African experiences of community, this African openness of spirit does not violate the right to privacy. I have frequently been impressed, in pastoral work in an African congregation, by the way in which Africans would avoid direct questions when trying to get at the truth of a matter. Furthermore, African colleagues were comfortable letting the persons involved select the time and manner in which they themselves chose to confess, rather than probing for a reluctant revelation of guilt. The conscience of a person is private and inviolable.

Similarly life is inviolable. It is God who gives life. To take life is a serious crime against life. Life is pre-eminently sacred. People in community are expected to work harmoniously towards the enhancement of life. Murder is the opposite of life enhancement. When blood is shed, the Nandi say explicitly, 'The ground is polluted'. They sacrifice ritually for the purification of the polluted land. The sacrifice is concluded by eating together, a sign that through the slaying of the sacrificial animal harmony has been restored and the community can now eat together again. The notion of the land being polluted by the shedding of blood is pervasive in Africa.[36]

16

Life is sacred, and its preservation is a sacred trust. In essence only God has the right to take life; 'God will judge me, not you', is a frequent expression which affirms that the person really does not have the right nor the authority to kill his fellow human being. To take away life is to violate the divine order; it is a serious and tragic perversion of God's life-giving intention for the person in community.

Murder is a flagrant violation of life. There are also other ways in which dehumanization unfolds. Envy, malice, anger, selfishness, pride, and arrogance are all attitudes which are dehumanizing and life-destroying. These evils of the spirit destroy people in community; they are life-destroying, a two-edged sword which destroys both the one who nurtures an evil attitude, and the one towards whom the evil is expressed. Therefore evil attitudes must be nipped in the bud. There is a profound awareness in African community that bitterness has a malevolence of its own which overpowers both the originator and many others as well. In extreme cases, the originator of the malevolence is regarded as a witch. It is imperative that the evil be snuffed out before it becomes a flame. It is for this reason that confession and restitution are built into the African experience of community.

Recently I participated in an African committee meeting where there was considerable hostility expressed toward one of the participants. It seemed that a stopper had been pulled. Out poured the angry words in a flow which went on and on. The person towards whom the hostility was expressed kept repeating over and over again, 'Thank you'! From his perspective the torrent of accusing words was good because he knew that unexpressed hostility becomes malignant. By expressing the angry inner attitudes, the whole group was experiencing a catharsis. Confession was a guarantee that the cancer of malevolence would be excised from the group. He realized that, by expressing its frustration and anger, the group was really saying that it did not want to destroy him or the group by permitting the wrong attitudes to fester.

I have worked closely with African colleagues for many years. Even in the office routine, every morning the greetings include enquiries about the welfare of my family. 'Did you sleep well?'

'How is the family?' 'Are the children well?' 'Is your wife well?' 'Is there peace in your home?' These are expressions of genuine concern; they grow out of the realization that the strain of office and work relationships could sow a seed of bitterness within me which might begin to poison my relationships at home. The potential for malevolence is always present. If all is well at home, then my office colleagues can assume that I had left the office the day before in peace, that by implication I was also at peace with those with whom I had worked, and therefore we could begin the day with a clean slate. If, on the other hand, there was trouble at home, then my work teammates would become very concerned and perhaps treat me more kindly than usual in the hope that the problem in my house would find its healing in the office routine. Sometimes I would be given a small gift and a word of encouragement when leaving the office in the evening. By returning home in peace, the evil which had invaded our home would leave.

Pride is also inimical to personhood. The proud person cannot mesh with community and he himself becomes a lesser person through his arrogance. Africans in community have beautiful techniques for helping the person maintain a proper perspective of himself, while at the same time not belittling him. An example is gift giving. If when offering a gift to one's friend, the receiver senses pride in the giver, the one who receives the gift may say with quiet but perceptive simplicity, 'Is this all that you are giving me!' If on the other hand the gift is given in humility, the recipient will express appreciation, but without sentimentality. The devices for affirmation, while at the same time negating egoism, are profound and subtle. The institution of dowry negotiations and gift exchanges in preparation for marriage, are, for example, exercises in personhood affirmation through gift sharing and receiving. Neither arrogance in generosity nor selfishness is permitted. The exchange of gifts is conducted in such a manner that all the participants feel affirmed but no one is allowed to boastfully feed his pride.

Bitterness as well as pride shrivel the person. We become small when we permit our spirits to be warped by attitudinal anger. The big person is the one who can live joyously without bitterness.[37] God, of course, is the truly Great Person. As we have mentioned earlier, among many African societies God is concerned about peace. For these peoples God-likeness is to be at peace. Ideally, as a person progresses through the life stages of birth, naming ceremony, puberty rites, marriage, and the further stages of maturity into eldership, he will progressively become a greater person. The trivial jealousies of childhood need to be abrogated as the person matures into greatness. Certainly the leaders among the elders, the sages of the community, are people who have demonstrated attitudinal maturity. Among the Gikuyu this is explicitly stated: the highest council of the society is the Congregation of Peace. These wise men have progressed through life's stages towards a deep awareness of the nature of life and the Life-Giver; they are the Council of Peace.[38]

The Council of Peace never affirmed punitive retribution. Punishment is always imposed for the purpose of enhancing the life of the person in community. Among the Abaluhya, if a man stole a cow because he was hungry, the likelihood was that little or no retribution would be imposed. A punishment which led to bitterness was counterproductive; the malevolence would be nurtured rather than snuffed out. Justice was for the preservation of life, not for its destruction.[39] Therefore the laws of justice were never codifiable. Justice was personal, not legalistic.

Justice also means that it is wrong for a destitute person to die of hunger. Social mores protected the rights of the destitute. For example, among the Embu, if one were hungry he was free to enter any garden and eat fruits and vegetables provided only that he did not carry any or run to hide if found eating in the garden.

Janheinz Jahn writes of an incident which illustrates the life-affirming characteristics of traditional person-oriented justice. Kapundwe's dog was found eating Busangu's sheep. The evidence indicated that the sheep had died naturally, and the dog then began eating the flesh of the dead sheep. Nevertheless, Kapundwe gave Busangu a sheep in restitution. Then he gave him a second sheep. Then a third. Then 100 francs. Why the apparent over-compensation? It was because Busangu said, 'I feel badly about my dead sheep'. Kapundwe and Busangu both realized that the pain from the loss of

19

the sheep could become malevolent, it could develop into bitterness. Neither wanted that to happen. The giving of compensation needed to continue until Busangu was at peace. That is the criterion for justice in traditional society. [40] Restitution is never imposed punitively. It is a process for the healing of relationships, for the affirmation of personhood, for the enhancement of life, the encouragement towards greatness.

Warfare is a tragic breakdown of community harmony. Probably it is for this reason that there has been ambiguity in African societies concerning God and warfare. Although some societies explicitly looked to God for victory in time of war, there was on the other hand an implicit hesitancy to presumptuously assume that God would bless the war. Some societies believed that war was a punishment from God for their sin. Others prayed to lesser deities, such as ancestral heroes, in time of war, but avoided requesting God's blessing on the enterprise. [41] At the time of the Gikuyu struggle for freedom in Kenya, the first Mau Mau oath was for unity, not violence. [42] Although violence did occur later, the prayers of the freedom fighters were not so much for the death of the enemy as for the establishment of peace and justice. [43] In one of Field Marshal Dedan Kimathi's recorded prayers offered in the forest camp of the freedom fighters, he says, 'Turn the enemies to be their friends . . . bless all our warriors wherever they may be.' [44]

God alone is the Life-Giver. To kill, even in warfare, is destructive invasion of life, although paradoxically war was sometimes recognized and accepted as expedient for the survival of the community. War was generally perceived as an unfortunate accident, which had to be quickly contained and peace re-established. Because life was sacred, the blood of those killed polluted the earth, making it necessary to cleanse the desecrated ground. As soon as possible elders congregated to cement the peace and the warriors participated in a sacrificial reconciliation meal. There were common reconciliation practices in time of warfare which we shall discuss in greater depth later.

Greatness is the capability to forgive. Jomo Kenyatta, founding father of the Kenyan nation and its first President, was acclaimed by

20

all as a truly great man. Although his presidency was flawed by several sad events, he knew how to forgive. His forgiveness of the white colonialists is particularly noteworthy. Many people anticipated that after Kenya gained independence all the white people would need to leave. But it was not so. Although Jomo Kenyatta had suffered bitterly under the colonial regime and had himself spent seven years in colonial detention during the Mau Mau war for freedom, he exercised the discipline of forgiveness. However, he cautioned that forgiveness did not necessarily mean forgetting. His book, *Suffering Without Bitterness, is* a testimony to the greatness of the man. Through his forgiveness, healing rather than malevolence characterized independent Kenya. Kenyatta was aware that bitterness would foster the cancer of dehumanization. He chose the more godly way of forgiveness, reconciliation and humanization.[45]

The humanization process which Jomo Kenyatta affirmed is an experience of joy and celebration. It is significant that in his quest to recapture traditional African culture, the aspect of culture mostly celebrated was the dance. During his last years this great man listened, probably daily, to choirs and troops of dancers who came to visit him from all parts of the Republic of Kenya. Dancing is about life. It is the celebration of the joy of living. Kenyatta perceived that the dance was a particularly significant sign of the life which flourishes when men and women learn to forgive one another and live in harmony with each other. Forgiveness enhances the dance of life. Dance is the celebration of the rich diversity of life, sorrow and joy, fear and courage, despair and hope.

Community and Humanity

Life is the gift of God. He is the nodal point, the originator and sustainer of life and peace. God's gift of life is only experienced authentically by people living in community. Because God is the nodal point of the person in community, life is organized hierarchically. God is the highest point in the pyramid of life. Life flows from him through the ancestral hero divinities, through the ancestral living dead, through the highest council of elders, through the various age sets of society until finally the life force of God

21

reaches even the womb where the unborn children are awaiting birth. From the moment of conception the new person begins his own personal pilgrimage in community through the stages of life towards that source of all life, who is God. He is the life giving source who unites the community and from whom all life proceeds and towards whom all life moves.[46]

Each respective community has its own systems of life enhancement, which are reinforced and nurtured by its respective hierarchy of the living and dead.[47] Within the hierarchical community structure, blessing flows from the nodal point down through the life pyramid. The nodal point is essentially impregnable. He is not affected by what mankind does. He blesses and shares the gift of life, but human aberration and sin do not generally affect God himself. There may be some exceptions, as for example the Baluba of Zaire who refer to God as 'the Bearer of Burdens' or as 'the Sorrowful or Suffering One'.[48] Nevertheless, although peace may not be possible when malevolence abounds in the community of people, in most African societies God himself is insulated from the evils which people do. God is not vulnerable to humankind.[49]

Yet God does preserve the community by providing the necessary gifts for the community to function. In any society, humankind is blessed with a variety of talents which are complementary and community affirming. The divine creation of the person in community with his complementary gifts for life enhancement is the theological base on which contemporary African philosophies of socialism are developed. Particularly in Tanzania the concern for *ujamaa* (familyhood) included an emphasis on a return to the land. It is the land which is God's special gift for the sustenance of life and community. It is within the earth's warm bosom that the living dead have been laid to rest. It is in contact with the earth that the ontocratic (a oneness encompassing divinity and nature or social organization; that is to say, divinity and social organization / nature have oneness. This is in contrast to the transcendent understanding of divinity, where divinity is other than nature or social organization). Relationship between God, the living dead, and the living is most perfectly experienced and expressed. The communion of human community

22

is earthly and practical. It is experienced in the rhythmic song of the men digging in the cassava patch and the hungry infant *muntu* receiving nourishment from the mother's breast.

The *ujamaa* villages of Tanzania attempted to utilize traditional decision-making process, which are a practical expression of the person in community. In these communities, decisions were made through the consensus process. African groups never vote; consensus is the manner for making decisions. After working within the African decision process for many years, I was horrified during a home leave in the United States at the manner in which a decision was made one evening in a Church council meeting. We were divided on an issue. Loud and conflicting voices were raised. Then, with feelings still high, we voted. The counted ballots confirmed that we were divided almost evenly. We left the meeting totally unhappy, and still divided between victors and vanquished. Never in Africa have I experienced that kind of split decision. If it is clear that the group is not united, the decision will be postponed for further reflection.

Authentic decision making in Africa is through the process of consensus. This process does not permit the humiliation and depersonalization of defeat. All must win through the process of right decision. Everyone has the opportunity to speak. As the eventual decision begins to emerge, the positions of the participants gradually shift until all are unanimous. No one leaves the group feeling that his opinion has not been heard. All have been affirmed. Personhood and community have been enhanced. African group processes never vote, because when a vote is cast, someone's opinion is defeated. It is the truth which unites the group and that truth cannot be determined by the vote. It is only perceivable through discussion and consensus.

African attitudes towards strangers are also a revelation of community. Although each African society has its own expressions of religion, there is the recognition that God is the creator of all peoples. Although the specific community is sacral, it is nevertheless not exclusive. Human community is both particular and universal, because God the creator is one. He is the creator of all peoples, and so all humankind are really one people. This insight has given the African people an enormous capability to affirm and welcome strangers. It is through hospitality to strangers that one shows his authentic participation in universal community, and he is thereby blessed. A visitor is a blessing.

The travelogues of the nineteenth century European explorers universally witness to the astonishing hospitality of the African peoples. Tragically some Europeans returned the courtesy with gunfire, and there were incidents of warfare between the explorers and the local populace. But investigation reveals that repeatedly, whenever hostilities erupted, it was because of treachery by the explorers or an inadvertent breach of peace etiquette. Even when hostilities did develop as during the Ashanti wars in Ghana, one is impressed by the gentleness of the Africans. In the siege of Kumasi in Ghana the Ashanti called a periodic truce to permit the British soldiers trapped in the garrison to come through the Ashanti lines to get water and provisions. Strangers, even if they be one's enemies, need to be treated as human beings!

Were there exceptions to the hospitality rule? Yes, there have been some. Africa has also had its 'Hitlers', butchers of peoples not of one's clan or race. But most African societies have never permitted racist or tribalistic Hitlers to survive for long. Racism is not an African contribution to humanity. The stranger is welcome!

Among the Gikuyu, hospitality to strangers was institutionalized by the strangers' granaries. Whenever the harvest was gathered, the community participated in a thanksgiving offering by putting aside a portion of the grain from each household for use by strangers. These gifts were offered to God for the strangers and were stored in little granaries at crossroads throughout the land of the Gikuyu. Whenever a stranger travelled through Gikuyu land, he was welcome to help himself to food from the granaries which stood at the intersections. Of course, if he was not in a hurry, he could also spend the night in the local homes, but for the person pressed for time, from one end of the country to another, the strangers' granaries were a welcome sign of Gikuyu hospitality. Food for the strangers was a thanksgiving offering to God.[50]

In a later chapter we will discuss covenant mechanisms for incorporating the permanent guest into a society forever. Because people are one creation under God, strangers were welcome, either temporarily or permanently. A friend has told me how in his childhood he remembers his father looking across the hills before eating the daily homestead meal to see if there might be any stranger passing by. If he saw someone, even a mile away, who appeared to be a traveller, he would run and call him to come and join in the meal. The guest was a blessing. He was a sign of the universality of human community. He was a sign that the local homestead was mystically intertwined with the whole world-wide community of human kind.

In this chapter we have reviewed the traditional African experience of man in community. The touchstone of truth, from an African traditionalist perspective, can only be found in a community. This is the heart cry of the Burundi Christian priest who was martyred for his faith. He writes:

> I see underdevelopment,
> I see religiosity.
> People sleep
> With a false hope.
> Formula of a faith not lived
> In the space time dimension
> Of integral development—
> Of the true Gospel.
>
> I see underdevelopment;
> I see religiosity,
> Tranquil consciences
> Satisfied hearts,
> Hey there!
> How does it happen
> That a brother is wounded?
>   is naked?
> Hey there!
> A brother is blind,
> does not know how to read
>   from the book
>   of technological life.[51]

JUSTICE, RECONCILIATION AND PEACE

REFERENCES

1. Malcolm J. McVeigh, *God in Africa, Concept of God in African Traditional Religion and Christianity,* Hartford, Claude Stark, 1974.
2. Placide Tempels, *Bantu Philosophy,* Paris, Presence Africaine, 1959.
3. Samuel G. Kibicho, 'The Gikuyu Conception of God, His Continuity into the Christian Era and the Question it Raises for the Christian Idea of Revelation', Unpublished Ph. D. dissertation, Nashville, Vandelbilt University, 1972.
4. E. Bolaji Idowu, *Olodumare, God in Yoruba Belief,* London, Longman, 1962.
5. John S. Mbiti, *Concepts of God in Africa,* London, S.P.C.K., 1970.
6. E.E.I. Evans Pritchard, *Nuer Religion,* Oxford, Oxford University Press, 1956.
7. Ibid., 14.
8. Ibid., 15.
9. Ibid., 16.
10. Jomo Kenyatta, *Facing Mount Kenya,* London, 1938, Reprinted by Mercury Books, 1961, 20-52.
11. Kibicho, op. cit., 16.
12. Ibid., 39.
13. Ibid, 33.
14. Ibid., 31, 53, 56-67.
15. Ibid., 57
16. Mbiti; op. cit., 40.
17. Ibid., 82, 83.
18. Ibid., 163.
19. Ibid., 36.
20. Ibid., 250.
21. Evans Pritchard, op. cit., 14,15,17,18, 25,177.
22. Ibid., 7, 9, 22.
23. Mbiti, op. cit., 250.
24. Idowu, op. cit., 47.
25. Tempels op. cit., 53.
26. Ibid.
27. John S. Mbiti, *African Religions and Philosophy,* London, Heineman 1971, 5.
28. Kenneth Kaunda, *Letter to My Children,* London, Longman 1973, 27.
29. John V. Taylor, *The Primal Vision,* London S.C.M. 1963, 99.
30. E. Bolaji Idowu, *African Traditional Religion, A Definition,* London S.C.M., 1973, 113.
31. Tempels, op.cit., 110.
32. Ibid. 107, 108.
33. Ibid. 54, 55.
34. Janheinz Jahn, *Muntu The New African Culture,* New York, Grove Press, Inc., 1961, 106, 107.
35. Tempels, op. cit., 105.
36. Kibicho, op. cit., 14.
37. Tempels, op. cit., 100.
38. Kibicho, op. cit., 14.
39. H.P. Junad, 'Reform of Penal Systems in Africa', *East African Law Journal,* vol. 2, no. 1, March, 1966, 31.
40. Jahn, op. cit, 116.
41. Mbiti, 78, 79.

42. Kibicho, op. cit., 266-8.
43. Renison Muchiri Githige, *The Religious Factor in Mau Mau with Particular reference to Mau Mau Oaths,* M.A. thesis, University of Nairobi, 1978, 280-305.
44. Kibicho, op. cit., 299-300.
45. Jomo Kenyatta, *Suffering Without Bitterness,* Nairobi, East African Publishing House, 1968.
46. Tempels, op. cit., 100.
47. Kibicho, op. cit., 197-198.
48. Mbiti, *Concepts of God in Africa,* 74.
49. Mbiti, *African Religions and Philosophy,* 208.
50. Margaret Kamau, 'Attitudes Towards Strangers in the Traditional Society and Within the Church', Nairobi, Kenyatta Universtity College Archives, n.d., 6.
51. Aylward Shorter, *African Christian Spirituality,* London Geoffrey Chapman, 1978, 51.

The slander of fools can injure honest men.
Friend, I gave you my trust, and you have repaid
By seeking to damage my name in the eyes of the tribe.
If ever there was love in me for you,
Now, by Allah, it is strangled and destroyed.
This is the way of life, this bitter way— —
Kindness towards men begets their secret hate.

Mohamed Abdullah Hassan
Somali Gabei

Chapter II

SUFFERING BECAUSE OF BROKEN RELATIONSHIPS

The Ba'ila of Zambia tell of an old woman who sought for God, the Besetting One (Leza). She was the daughter of tragedy. She was orphaned in childhood. As she grew older her relatives also died, and then her children, and then also her grandchildren. She was completely alone. Why, she asked, has Leza afflicted me so?

She was determined to find Leza to ask him the cause of her tragic sadness and aloneness. She knew that Leza must dwell in the sky, and so she built a tower of wood to reach into the heavens. She tried again and again, but each tower failed to take her high enough to reach Leza.

Then she struck on a better plan. In the far horizon the old woman observed that the sky met the earth. Surely there in the distance Leza could be found, at the place where his heavenly abode met the earth. And so with keen anticipation the old woman set out on a journey towards the horizon to find Leza and seek the answer to the perplexities of death and tragedy in her family. Day after day she walked, past one country and another.

As she passed along her way towards the horizon, the strange people whom she passed would ask, 'Old woman, where are you going?'

And she replied, 'I am going to find Leza to learn from him the reason for death and tragedy'.

On and on and on the old woman travelled. She never found Leza.[1]

Disharmony in Community

This story of the Ba'ila woman's quest for Leza reveals a perplexity concerning God and his relationship to the human community which is repeated in various forms through story and myth across the African continent. Although life and peace in community is idealized, there is a persistent recognition that people fail to fully experience that life. 'We are but men' is a typical African expression of resignation and confession of the frailty and failure of humankind to experience life fully and joyously.[2] A profound aspect of the myths of mortality is the notion that community has been distorted, has become death prone, because something has gone wrong between the Creator and humankind. This theological notion is somewhat similar to Biblical and Quranic insights, and consequently some scholars speculate that these myths of separation between God and humankind are a reflection of Christian or Islamic theological intrusion into traditional African perceptions. Nevertheless, the widespread persistence of these myths in widely variegated form does not seem to support a Biblical or Quranic origin. Over two thousand myths of the creation and original state of humankind have been identified by H. Baumann.[3] These myths are authentic African insights into the nature of the human situation.[4]

We shall mention only two other myths here from this wide selection. The Ashanti of Ghana tell of God's benevolent presence among his people after the creation. God was so close that a woman pounding her food with the pestle sometimes hit him. For this reason God began to withdraw from people. Higher and higher into the sky he went. The woman was terrified, and gathered all the village mortars together and stacked them one on top of the other in order to reach God. Finally the tower of mortars was within only one mortar of reaching him; in her haste and excitement she seized the mortar at the bottom of the pile to put it on the top, and the whole mortar tower came tumbling down. God could not be reached! He was separated from people forever.

Some of the people of the White Nile Valley in Sudan believe that in the past God was united with people by a rope which linked heaven and earth together. God frequently descended from heaven and dwelt with people in peace and blessing. Then the hyena chewed the rope off, and thereafter earth and heaven have been permanently severed.[5]

In some of the myths of separation there is the suggestion that God is to blame. In others the separation took place accidentally, or because of the misfortune of fate, or because of man's disobedience or importunity. Whatever the case may be, in all the myths of separation, irreparable harm is the consequence for human community.[6] John S. Mbiti surveys several examples of the magic results of the separation. He summarizes his findings thus:

And so the original direct contact and relationship between God and man was broken. The unfortunate consequences for man include the loss of immortality, resurrection, rejuvenation, and free food, in addition to the coming of death and suffering.[7]

The myths of separation also affirm that there is no healing possible for the separation. The God who is separated will never return, and no tower built by man will ever reach high enough to recapture the primal relationship between God and man. Mbiti says,

It is remarkable that out of these many myths concerning the primeval man and the loss of his original state, there is not a single myth, to my knowledge, which even attempts to suggest a solution or reversal of this great loss.[8]

The 'golden age' of beautiful life-giving relationships is gone forever. The person shall die. His communities are not reflections of perfect harmony. Evil and death become reality. We are but people.[9]

The most obvious evidence of broken harmony is the unpredictableness of nature. The land, which God has given to people for life, often robs people of the very life which we so desperately desire. Violent storms level the crops. Alternatively parched soil will shrivel the harvest, even though people toil desperately to squeeze sustenance from the earth.

Disease and plague are also evidence that harmony is broken. In totemic societies, even that sacred sign of the harmony between humankind and nature does not always relate affirmingly in relationship to his human kinsmen. The totem may, on occasion, even turn against his own descendents. Humankind and nature are estranged.

But no aspect of African community life so tragically illustrates the deadly nature of broken relationships as witchcraft and sorcery. The witch or sorcerer is a person who is consumed by either anger or envy, one who feeds on broken relationships. There is no greater terror than the awareness that a relationship seems irreparable, because broken harmony is the seedbed of death.[10] The witch is the irredeemable one, who has nurtured malevolence in his spirit and turned that malevolence against his fellowpersons. The power of his evil intent does kill; it is death incarnate.[11] It is for this reason that when a witch or sorcerer was identified, some African societies were merciless in vengeance. Among the Meru of Kenya, he was placed in a beehive! He had to die to exorcise the cancer of hate and death in society. More often, however, there were attempts to cleanse the witch of his intentions.[12] A witch who confessed witchcraft could be readopted into his community.

Although the witch is the epitome of evil, the incarnation of death, the revelation of the deathness of a broken community, he is not the only manifestation of disharmony. Somewhat akin to witchcraft is the experience of spirit possession. I.M. Lewis points out that spirit possession is often compensatory for status which one has been deprived of within his community.[13] It is for this reason that spirit possession is particularly common among women in societies which seem to be excessively patriarchal. Okot p'Bitek seems to affirm Lewis in his description of cases of possession created through anxiety.[14] M. Singleton describes several cases of spirit possession caused by anxiety which he met in his pastoral ministry in Tanzania.

First was a woman whose husband bought himself a new outfit, but neglected to give his wife her annual gift of a new dress. Shortly thereafter the woman became possessed with an evil demon of judgmentalism towards her husband. Exorcism was possible only after the husband and wife had become reconciled and her anxieties concerning her husband's commitment to her were allayed.

Second was a woman who worked as a shopkeeper in her husband's store. She inadvertently angered her husband by selling on credit to a neighbourhood housewife. When the creditor learned of the husband's anger, she sent a peace offering of a chicken which the husband angrily threw to the dog, suspecting that it might have been laced with poison. His shopkeeper wife became very ill. The problem was diagnosed as possession. The diviners recommended that the creditor be removed from the neighbourhood to effectuate cleansing. A happier solution was found by bringing reconciliation between all three parties involved: the husband, the wife, and their neighbour. Then the evil spirit was easily exorcised.[15]

In both cases, spirit possession occurred because of broken relationships. The exorcism of the demon could not proceed until the problems affecting relationships were resolved. The demons were symptomatic. The cure needed to go behind the symptoms to the death creating phenomenon which preceded the possession experience.

Witchcraft and spirit possession are only two examples of death and dehumanization which is created through broken relationships. Jealousy and envy are common human experiences which are expressed in a multitude of dangerous ways, which are only proportionately less dangerous than witchcraft. These evils are also feared. For example, many times Africans have told me that the greatest deterrent to good relationships is malicious gossip. Speaking unkindly about one's fellow poisons the relationship between people, and everyone suffers. Relational evils such as gossip pour forth from the inner springs of wounded man, who has not been great enough to confront injustice, redress the wrong, and forgive. The person who does not forgive degenerates into smallness; he may even become a murderer. This propensity to smallness is evil, subhuman. As the Akan say, man himself is prone to evil.[16] Disharmony is common to man in community. The 'golden age' is in the past; it cannot be fully recovered. Community today can only be an imperfect reflection of the ideal.[17]

Nevertheless, aspects of the ideal can be recaptured through social and religious devices. African traditional religion is intensely concerned with the attempt to recreate and maintain social harmony in the present, and although the myths of origin reveal that the ideal of perfect relationships is not recoverable, there are many spiritual devices available which attempt to help the person in community regain and maintain aspects of the paradise lost.[18] We shall now look briefly at some of these harmony- and life-maintaining devices.

A Quest for Harmony

In this chapter we shall briefly discuss only three ways in which African peoples have attempted to recapture aspects of the life-enhancing harmony of the 'golden age'. The next chapter will describe covenant as a means for recreating broken relationships, but in this chapter we note the life-sustaining role of progeny, hierarchy and sacrifice. Our discussion is cursory, for these salvatory dimensions of African religion have been deeply probed by scholars such as John S. Mbiti and E. Bolaji Idowu.

PROGENY

We have mentioned that many African myths of origin suggest that mortality is one of the consequences of the separation between God and man. The quest to recapture immortality by regaining the presence of God is impossible. None of the mythical towers ever reached high enough to find God; the Ba'ila woman never found the place where the sky touched the earth. Nevertheless, through progeny an aspect of the lost immortality is recaptured. It is believed that as long as one is remembered, his personhood is preserved. Personal life after death is assured if one is remembered.

Children are therefore person-affirming and life-enhancing. Through offspring one acquires personal stature and security in this life and personal survival after death. Biological offspring are exceedingly significant. Nevertheless, even for the childless there is hope, a hope derived from participation in normal kinship responsibilities. Even one's brothers' children can become one's own, through kinship loyalties.

The need to be remembered after one dies means that marriage and the begetting of children are soteriological. The purpose of marriage is progeny, who will provide for one in old age and remember one after death through libations and sacrifice. One who has no children or kinsmen is truly lost. When he dies he will be cut off forever from the stream of life. Unremembered, he will drift into oblivion and nothingness. It is only through children that oblivion can be averted, life after death is assured, and one's position in kinship and community is secured. Children are the guarantee that the lost immortality is not a total loss. Through children the sacredness of life is affirmed and secured, both in the present and in death.[19]

HIERARCHY OF LIFE

The hierarchy of power and life is a second and closely related means for recapturing aspects of the lost harmony and enhancing the sacredness of life. The base of the hierarchical pyramid are the unborn who are nourished in the loins of the people. The apex of the hierarchy is God. The hierarchy is theologically sustained. Although God might have moved away from humankind, he is not altogether unknown. African life has always been saturated with personal prayer expressions to God.[20] Especially in times of calamity, he is addressed in communal prayers. God is addressed in prayer because he is the nodal point from whom life flows and to whom life returns. Although remote, he is not absent. The hierarchy of powers, therefore, is the ontological linkage between God and human society. Through the hierarchy, unity, harmony, and life are sustained by God.[21]

Between the apex and the base of the hierarchy there are many stages of ascendency. The first step up the hierarchical pyramid is conception. Through conception the incipient life in the loins has begun to take form. The birth and naming ceremony are a further development in the formation of personhood. The naming ceremonies in some societies are exceedingly significant as person-affirming rituals.[22] We have already mentioned the great importance of the name in expressing the uniqueness of the person in a community.

Puberty rites are a further stage upward in the life pyramid. Many African societies circumcise both the male and female at puberty. Regardless of what the outward sign of the puberty rites might be, the whole ceremony is an institution of incorporation into the community as an adult. The young person enters the rites as a child; he or she is an adult when the rites are completed. During the rites the sages of the society teach the initiates the inner secrets of the society, the values by which the people live, the traditions, myths, and lore which are the sacral nourishment of the community. The values of the society are reinforced by pain, the pain of the circumcision incision or the removal of teeth or other forms of bodily and spiritual pain and discipline. The reinforcement of values by pain inscribes these values deeply and they are never forgotten.[23]

The dramatic change from childhood to adulthood is often accompanied by the acquisition of a new name. Many societies refer to this transition as a new birth, and the new name is a sign of this profound metamorphosis from the frivolities of childhood to the responsibilities of adulthood. The new birth is a covenant of incorporation into the community.[24] In many societies the covenant is mystically sealed by the circumcision blood which flows into the ground thereby uniting forever the newborn person with the life sustaining force of the ancestral living dead. Through the new birth covenant of incorporation, the initiated person has been summoned into full participation in the family of humankind. The circumcision covenant blood has provided him with access to resources of life power which a child could not comprehend.[25]

Marriage is the next stage. In the following chapters we shall discuss marriage in greater depth in the context of covenant. In marriage salvation becomes effectuated, for it is through marriage that new persons are created, that life is transmitted and the continuity of a community assured. The life enhancement of marriage is twofold: first, the parents contribute to the continuity of a living community through their progeny. Second, the children sustain the life of their parents by nurturing them in old age and remembering them in death. While the puberty rite is the incorporation into adulthood, marriage is potential incorporation into immortality.

From marriage through old age, the person moves through various stages of increasing responsibility. In many societies these steps upward in the power hierarchy are thoroughly institutionalized. Among the Gikuyu there have been elaborate handing over ceremonies of symbols of power as the elders move upward from one stage of authority to another. The eldest are the most highly respected, for they have reached the stage wherein they are the closest, among the living, to the nodal point of life. Among the Gikuyu this highest congregation of elders is called the Council of Peace. They are the ones entrusted with the awesome responsibility of assuring the harmony and peace of the community.[26]

In some traditional societies a chief or king became the apex of power. He was the link between the living dead and the living, between God and humankind.[27] In his personhood the life and harmony of the community were assured. Any violation of his personhood was therefore also a violation of community and life itself.

The traditional appreciation of the hierarchical unity of the community significantly affects modern African political structures. It is for this reason that most modern African states are exceedingly uncomfortable having more than one person running for president. The national political apparatuses are sufficiently attuned to consensus that only one candidate actually runs for presidential office. Harmony is the key to life. Divisive campaigns for the key office in the land would be seriously disruptive to life and freedom. Unified leadership is the key to community harmony and life.

I was impressed with the manner in which the Republic of Kenya selected the next president after the death of President Kenyatta in 1978. The whole nation participated in an exercise of consensus formation. Out of the consensus, process, one name emerged. The actual election, then, became the confirmation of that one whom many by consensus had already selected; it was a celebration of affirmation.

The head of the community incorporates the unity of that community. In him harmony and life are secured. Any form of malevolence to his personhood is in fact the dehumanization of the community as a whole. The hierarchy of power and life is for peace.

Death is the stage of transition from the condition of living to that of the living dead. The living dead are the people who have moved a stage closer to the source of life than the living, and hence they have ascended in the hierarchy of life power. The living dead ancestors are highly respected, and in traditional society they were invited to participate with the living in all of life's activities. Libations and sacrifices were offered as invitations to the living dead to be beneficially present. In many societies the living dead are hierarchically conceived, just as is true in the society of the living. Some of the ancestral heroes might become divinities who are worshipped, but this is not universally so in Africa.[28] In East Africa it is doubtful that the Gikuyu veneration of ancestors ever became worship, yet among the Baganda of Uganda a hierarchy of divinities was a pronounced aspect of the cult of the Kabakaship.

We have surveyed the hierarchy of power in a generalized manner. There are fascinating variations within all of Africa's societies. Some nomadic cultures have never had a distinct power hierarchy. Some few societies are sufficiently egalitarian that even the life stages have not been institutionalized. Nevertheless, in most of sub-Saharan Africa the power hierarchy is life affirming because it secures community harmony and it is the pyramid of life and power which has its source in God

We have described the hierarchy vertically. Although African myths do often refer to God as being in the sky, they also speak of the living dead as being in the earth. Therefore, a tiered or spatial cosmology is not fully adequate for describing the power configuration of African societies. Professor Mbiti describes the hierarchy from the perspective of time; God created people and stayed close to people at the creation. That was the 'golden age'. Life in the present is caused by that creative beginning. The person comes from the past *(zamani)* and returns into the *zamani*. As one progresses through the life stages, one is moving from the present *(sasa)* into the *zamani*. It is relative proximity to *zamani* which gives one authentic access to power and life.

The present is blessed by its links with the *zamani*, and the present generation in turn is progressing into the *zamani*. The greatness of a person is, therefore, not his elevation in space, but his perception of *zamani*, his spiritual proximity to the ancestral living dead, and even his realization of the mystery of God who in the beginning created humankind.[29]

Although the power hierarchy, whether conceived either spatially or temporally, sustains harmony and stability, malevolence is still a persistent problem. Harmony is only imperfectly achievable, and tragic breakdown in community relationships is always possible. When harmony breaks down, sacrifice is often made to attempt to recreate harmony. We turn now to sacrifice as a third dimension of the African quest for a recovery of aspects of the primal life enhancing experiences of harmony.

SACRIFICE

In traditional society sacrifice was an exceedingly significant means through which society attempted to re-establish harmony and preserve life.[30] In traditional African societies sacrifices were normally performed in response to exigencies or as part of the yearly harvest cycle. Sacrifices on behalf of the living dead were performed by a household, and sacrifices to God or the divinities were performed by the entire community. There is a mystery concerning the meaning of sacrifices. Mbiti mentions four theories: gift, propitiation, communion and thank-offering. Perhaps all four are involved. The fundamental purpose of the sacrifice is the preservation or recreation of harmony.[31]

Mbiti writes:

One may add that an ontological balance must be maintained between God and man, the spirits and man, the departed and the living. When this balance is upset, people experience misfortunes and sufferings, or fear that these will strike them. The making of sacrifice and offerings, on the other hand, is also a psychological device to restore this ontological balance. It is also an act and occasion of making and renewing contact between God and man, the spirits and man, i.e., the spiritual and the physical worlds. When these acts are directed towards the living dead, they are a symbol of fellowship, a recognition that the departed are still members of their human families, and tokens of respect and remembrance for the living dead.[32]

Normally the sacrifice had to be preceded by confession and cleansing of all forms of evil. Among the Rendille of Kenya there is a great communal sacrifice once every fifteen years. These nomadic goat-herders congregate for days before the sacrifice to confess all the evil which has accumulated during the previous years. Where wrongs have occurred, there is restitution. After all has been uncovered and confessed, and harmony has been established through the community, there is a great sacrificial feast. This is also the time for marriage. The harmony which has been established through confession, restitution and sacrifice is affirmed through marriage and sexual union.

When the sacrificial animal is eaten, it is normally the case in many African societies that those who do not have clean hearts should absent themselves. To eat of the animal with malice is a serious form of hypocrisy which would be selfdestructive. Cleansing before the sacrifice might involve confession, but it also might be ritually performed by symbolically spitting out one's anger. When someone feels anger gripping him, spitting is a common practice in many societies. The anger is symbolically spat out, so that one can become freed from its tentacles. Vomiting out malice is also practised in some places. Whatever the technique, cleansing of evil attitudes is a prerequisite for sacrifice. Those who are not clean inside cannot participate.[33]

The eating of the sacrificial animal is a communion and a celebration of harmony and life. Among the Gikuyu the various parts of the animal are eaten by different groups in the community thereby sacramentally symbolizing both their personal individuality and their union in communion in the sacrificial feast. The elders eat the head; the jaw is for the friends who have joined in the sacrifice; the first cervical vertebra with the surrounding flesh are for the poor and elderly; the family inlaws receive the foreleg, stomach, sausage, liver, intestine, meat from the shoulder and the tail; the young people are given the gland, sausage and small intestine; young girls are given kidneys, tendons, and ears so that they will listen well when they marry; the young boys receive the neck; the womenfolk eat the small stomach, small intestines, liver, sausage, and tail; respected and wealthy people in the community get the chest, oesophagus, ribs, sausage, and the front legs. Everyone has a part! The feasting on the sacrificial animal is a powerful sign of personhood and the unity of the community. In sacrificing and eating the roasted animal together, the community is recreated and confirmed. As the Gikuyu say, 'You can never eat a goat alone!' It must be eaten in fellowship.[34]

Progeny, hierarchy, and sacrifice—these three themes are exceedingly important in the African quest for harmony and life in a community. Although the person is only a person, although God may not be as presently near as he once was, although the gift of immortality escapes the human quest, yet there is still a way for the person to attempt to maintain aspects of life nourishing harmony. The birth of children who perpetuate the life of the community, the hierarchy of life which provides life-enhancing unity, and the sacrificial system through which malevolence can be cleansed, these themes all help to maintain harmony in traditional society. Yet they are not sufficient. The forces of disunity have prevailed too frequently. Perhaps it is for this reason that African societies developed another exceedingly significant practice in their attempt to maintain unity. This is the practice of covenant. We turn now to that important aspect of the African quest for the harmony of the person in community.

JUSTICE, RECONCILIATION AND PEACE

REFERENCES

1. Malcolm J. Mc Veigh, *God in Africa*, Hartford, Claude Stark, 1974, 48, 49.
2. John S. Pobee, *Toward an African Theology*, Nashville, Abingdon, 1979, 112, 113
3. H. Baumann, *Schopfung und Urzeit des Menschen im Mythus der Afrikanischen Volker*, Berlin, Reimer, Second Edition, 1974.
4. Mc Veigh, op. cit., 53, 54.
5. John S. Mbiti, *African Religions and Philosophy*, London, Heineman, 1971, 97.
6. Ibid.
7. Ibid., 98, 99.
8. John S. Mbiti, *Concepts of God in Africa*, London, S.P.C.K. 1970, 177.
9. Mbiti, *African Religions and Philosophy*, 98.
10. Pobee, op. cit, 112, 113.
11. Okot p'Bitek, *Religion of the Central Luo*, Nairobi, E.A.L.B., 1971, 123, 147.
12. Pobee, op.cit.,114-116.
13. Mbiti, *African Religions and Philosophy*, 201-3.
14. I.M. Lewis, *Ecstatic Religion*, Baltimore, Penguin, 1971.
15. p'Bitek, op. cit., 114.
16. M. Singleton, 'Ancestors, Adolescents, and the Absolute, An Exercise in Contextualisation', *Pro Mundi Vita Bulletin*, 68, September-October, 1977.
17. Pobee, op. cit., 108, 119.
18. Mbiti, *African Religions and Philosophy*, 98, 99.
19. Ibid.
20. Ibid., 133, 134
21. Ibid., 61-66.
22. E. Bolaji Idowu, *African Traditional Religion*, London, S.C.M., 1973, 137-89.
23. Mbiti, *African Religions and Philosophy*, 118-20.
24. Ibid., 121-32.
25. Kwesi Dickson and Paul Ellingworth, *Biblical Revelation and African Beliefs*, Maryknoll, Orbis, 1969, 137-145. Mbiti, 121-132.
26. Jomo Kenyatta, *Facing Mount Kenya*, London, 1938, reprinted by Mercury Books, 1961, 130-62.
27. Kenyatta, op. cit., 186-205
28. Pobee, op. cit., 95
29. Mbiti, *African Religions and Philosophy*, 75-91
30. Ibid., 15-28
31. Mbiti, *Concepts of God in Africa*, 177
32. Ibid., 178, 179
33. Mbiti, *African Religions and Philosophy*, 59
34. Monica Wilson, *Religions and the Transformation of Society*, Cambridge, Cambridge University Press, 1971, 64-6.
35. Joram Mwangi and several Gikuyu elders, informants.

Hey you people!
Wake up in your home, if you are there.
Hey, Ndele, drink this beer!
You people, if you are there in this compound,
Take this beer.
Mlangali, drink this beer at your compound.
Nkalanga, beer!
Mwagamba, you too, if you are here.
You who are in the white place,
We are here in your compound.
We are disappearing because of disease.
We have come here, you people.

Safwa of Tanzania

> (A celebrative prayer for renewed
> relationships between the living
> and the living dead.)

Chapter III

COVENANTS FOR JUSTICE,
RECONCILIATION AND PEACE

Amin was a Batire orphan. A missionary friend of mine, an elderly gentleman, received the orphaned Amin into his home. An informal father-son relationship developed. From Amin's perspective he became an adopted son.

Then Amin's adopted father died. Amin was devastated. He came to my home and explained that he belonged to my clan. Adoption is forever.

When I told him that I could not fulfil the obligations of being his adoptive parent, he was appalled. He was incredulous that the rights of adoption could be affected by the death of only one elder. He knew that he belonged to my clan eternally, for he had been adopted.

Adoption is a form of irrevocable covenant. We have seen that traditional African religion has developed socio-religious devices for attempting to enhance or recreate harmony in the community. Covenant is the deepest and most profound level of personal and community recreation. It involves a much deeper level of commitment than is assumed in a contract. In African societies covenant is a commitment to one another which is grounded in communal-religious ontology. Within the traditional African approach to covenant there is a sincere and earnest commitment to perfecting human relationships. Good relationships are made better, broken relationships are renewed, and new relationships are created. Through covenant, harmony is restored and affirmed. The community is reborn; it springs forth joyously recreated from the primordial womb of creation.

It is impossible to adjudge to what extent the traditional African experience of God-man covenant has been informed by Biblical or Quranic themes. Both Christianity and Islam were planted in North Africa at the time of their respective origins.

44

Furthermore, the fringes of tropical Africa have been exposed to Islam for over a thousand years, and Christianity has been interacting with coastal communities for five hundred years. During the past century all of interior sub-Saharan Africa has been tremendously influenced by the modern expansion of Christian and Muslim mission. It is thus impossible to accurately ascertain what is purely indigenous and what has been borrowed. Nevertheless, the African traditional heritage possesses a resiliency which makes tentative judgements feasible concerning the original African perception. The evidence suggests that some perceptions of God in covenant with man have always been present within the African experience.

Although man's experience of covenant with God is frequently obscured, especially in societies where divine or ancestral mediators play an important role, in many other societies across the African continent hints of God in covenant are discernible. The importance and universality of both communal and man to man covenants strongly suggest an original theological undergirding centred on man's covenant with God. In other words, covenant in Africa seems to be at least subliminally derived from God, who is the source of personal harmony. Although the primal harmony between God and man may have been distorted through accident, fate, or human frailty, God has not left himself without a witness.

Devices for renewed covenant are available. God has not left people in complete darkness; he has not forsaken them altogether; he does wish to bless his people, but the blessing is contingent on people's obedience to God as expressed in the hierarchical power configuration. Misfortune is evidence of disharmony; it reveals that the person has either willingly or inadvertently gone astray. Penance, often in the form of a propitiatory sacrifice, is required to restore equilibrium and harmony. Through obedience to divinity as expressed in hierarchical power, the blessing of covenant is renewed.[2]

The term 'covenant' for the God-man relationship must be used cautiously. The Biblical understanding of Yahweh, the God of covenant who reveals himself in righteous personal encounter with man calling people to repentance, is not found in any other religious heritage. Yahweh in covenant is uniquely Biblical. Neverthelss, within many non-Biblical traditions, hints of God-man covenants are present. The way of devotion in the Hindu Bagavad Gita or the Boddisatvas of Greater Vehicle Buddhism are examples of a quest for restored harmony and blessing appropriate to divinity. The African heritage contains similar covenant hints.

Seeking God's Favour

We shall examine two examples of seeking God's favour derived from the Bantu Gikuyu of central Kenya and the Nilotic Luo of western Kenya. These two societies are selected advisedly: first because they are representative of the widely dispersed Nilotic and Bantu societies, and secondly because there is considerable indigenous research available. Following our description of traditional Gikuyu and Luo efforts to seek divine favour, we shall describe examples of interpersonal and intercommunity covenants in a number of East African societies.

THE GIKUYU

The ancient Gikuyu name for God is *Mugai* or *Ngai,* which means the Divider of the Universe. According to the Gikuyu myth of origin, after God created Mount Kenya (Kirinyaga) and the surrounding land, he gave Gikuyu and Mũmbi (the ancestors of the Gikuyu people) the land which was to be theirs forever. The primal couple settled beneath a luxuriant *mugumo* (fig) tree. When he gave them their land, he also promised that whenever there was need they should sacrifice and raise their hands towards snowcapped Kirinyaga (the mountain which shines mysteriously). Then God would aid them. The covenant was straightforward. God gave the Gikuyu their land and he would continue to bless them if they worshipped him appropriately. God soon blessed the primal pair with nine daughters, but they had no husbands.

God made it known to Gikuyu and Mumbi that he would bless their daughters with husbands if the parents sacrificed in a manner pleasing to God: one kid and one lamb were needed for sacrifice under a fig tree, the blood and the fat of which would be poured on the trunk. The meat would be burnt in sacrifice, and prayers would be offered. Thereafter God miraculously created nine young men who became the husbands of the nine daughters of Gikuyu and Mumbi.[3]

Normally the traditional Gikuyu avoided disturbing God. Their saying: *Ngai ndagiagiagwo* (God should not be pestered) succinctly expresses their attitude. But in times of calamity, when all else had failed, they did beseech God in the appropriate manner. Not only was sacrifice and worship necessary, but the society also needed to determine the causes of the disaster. For this they turned to their seers who had been selected and ordained to comprehend the mystery of God. Such comprehension was necessary in order to receive revelation concerning what offences the people had committed. The 'seeing' of the mystery was dramatized in the ordination ceremony, when the initiate was required to cover his eyes with the fatty lining of a sacrificed he-goat, and then a small hole was cut in the tissue through which he could symbolically peek into the mysteries of God.[4] These seers were required to reveal to the people the mystery, the reason for a calamity, such as failure of the rains.

After the mystery was revealed, the society attempted to put matters right. That which had defiled the society had to be dealt with; confession and restitution techniques might be needed. The seers also revealed the kind of animal which should be sacrificed. Several highly respected elders noted for integrity, and a young boy and a girl who were still innocent, were chosen to conduct the sacrifice. As the day of sacrifice approached, all forms of dancing or war-like activities were renounced. Each family emphasised only that which promoted peace. Harmony in the community was essential for the renewal of communion with God. The sacrificial day had to be peaceful, for God is the God of peace and blessing. Even the selection of the sacrificial animal reflected the moral-harmony theme of the event. The man himself, whose lamb was selected, had to be a righteous man who had never committed theft, murder, rape, or witchcraft. God only accepted the sacrifice of the righteous.

The sacrifice itself was performed under the sacred *Mugumo* tree, whose size and perennial foliage symbolized the abundant life of God. It was in a grove of these trees that the primal couple were first commanded to make their homes. It was similarly within the shade of this *Mugumo* tree that the person returned to his maker in penitence and sacrifice for renewed communion and blessing.[5]

Just as the *Mugumo* tree symbolically represented God, so did the select elders and two children represent the community. God and people symbolically met at the *Mugumo* tree. The ancestral living-dead were also present for they were the keepers of the sacred tree. The sacrifice of honey beer, milk, and lamb represented life, nourishment and joy. Symbolically God himself provided the fire with which to accept the sacrifice, for it was only with sticks from the sacred tree that the fire could be lighted. The communion motif was highlighted by the participants feasting together under the sacred tree, while offering sacrifice to God and libations to the living-dead. Eating in the presence of God and the living-dead was the epitome of harmony and blessing. The ritual prayers were punctuated with the repetitive chorus, 'Peace, we beseech you, *Ngai*, peace be with us'.[6] Communion is peace. Harmony is blessing.

In traditional religious experience, God seems to have honoured these sacrifices. Many Gikuyu sages tell of God blessing the land with rain after the sacrifices were offered. The blessing of rain after sacrifice was a perpetual reminder that God would never break his covenant with the Gikuyu people. God does bless when the community confesses its sins, makes restitution, and offers appropriate sacrifice and worship.[7]

THE CENTRAL AND SOUTHERN LUO

Among the Luo of western Kenya, the covenant motif is not as explicitly developed as seems to be the case among the Gikuyu. Probably this is because of the diffusion of the Luo peoples due to their pastoral migrations. Yet there is the persistent theme of returning to 'God' for renewal of harmony and blessing. The persistence of the renewal theme may be an echo of covenant awareness.

Professor Okot p'Bitek describes participation in the annual festival of *Jok* at Baka Hill.[8] Among the Central Luo – otherwise known in Uganda as Lwoo or Acholi in contrast to the "Southern Luo" of Kenya and Tanzania – the *Jok* were spirits. p'Bitek believed that the notion of one God whose power is manifested through the *Jok* was not part of the Luo traditional cosmology.[9] On the other hand, however, Evans-Pritchard seems to have established that the spirit divinities *(Kwoth)* of the Nilotic Nuer and Dinka are signs of God who is over all.[10] It seems highly doubtful that the traditional Luo would have been an exception to the monotheistic milieu of their Nilotic kinsmen and other East African neighbours, as though the Jok were particularized manifestations of divinity, certainly God *(Nyasai* or *Nyasaye)* was perceived as the power beyond the *Jok.*

Each chieftain was associated with a *Jok* shrine. Annually there was a pilgrimage to the shrine. The priests were responsible to lead the people in the pilgrimage. For weeks and even months before the pilgrimage, people throughout the chieftainship concerned themselves with confession and restitution. All evil and malice had to be put away. Peace had to be established throughout the domain. Inter-clan feuds were examined, the causes determined, and appropriate steps taken to end the feuds. In some situations where unusual misfortunes had prevailed, the priest was requested to determine the causes of the trouble. Usually the priest identified evils such as malice within the group. The evil had to be cleansed before the community could consider approaching the sacred shrine. Peace was required before the clan could approach God.

On the day of the festival representatives from the entire chiefdom began the pilgrimage to the sacred hill Baka, where there was a cave which was the abode of a *Jok.* Animals and delicacies were taken for sacrifice and feasting. On the way the *Jok* himself provided an *oribi* as his contribution to the feast. Also the sacrificial goat broke its string and fled to the cave ahead of the procession, and when they arrived the *Jok* had already slain the goat in preparation for the sacrifice. After the animals were slain and the food prepared, morsels were thrown into the cave to feed the *Jok,* and the priest prayed:

Our insides are clean,
we have brought you food with clean insides
Eat it . . .[11]

The prayer continued, beseeching blessing. It is significant that the prerequisite to blessing was 'clean inside'. It is clear from the preparations which preceded the feast that 'clean' meant moral integrity.

After the *Jok* had accepted the sacrifice (and certainly the slain goat found at the mouth of the cave when the congregation arrived was a sign that the *Jok* was pleased with the sacrifice), the congregation was sprinkled with earth from the cave. Thereafter feasting began and then a mock fight took place symbolizing the destruction of all malevolence. The festival concluded with a joyous procession returning to the chief's home. At the entrance another mock fight took place. The residents who did not go along on the pilgrimage attempted to prevent the pilgrims from entering the chief's enclosure, but they were overcome; this symbolized the power of the blessing of the *Jok* overcoming that which would prevent blessing. The adversary having been 'defeated', the congregation entered the chief's homestead where they feasted and danced. Later the clans dispersed to their respective centres where the feasting and dancing continued all night.'[12]

The themes which dominate in this renewal experience are confession, congregational sacrifice, feasting in the presence of the *Jok,* defeating evil, celebration and joy. Annually the entire society participated in this renewal event. The chieftainship was blessed through the reaffirmation of appropriate relationship with *Jok.* Similarly any deliberate or careless lack of respect for *Jok* was seriously malevolent. Only when Jok was properly respected and appeased did he bless the chieftainship.

We have described the traditional Acholi and Gikuyu renewal phenomena as examples of seeking the favour of God within the African traditional heritage. Some may suggest these sacrificial rites are examples of hints of divine-human covenant. Probably this is true. Nevertheless, certain cautions are needed. Traditional African religion could not contemplate a genuine covenant with God, for covenants were only possible between equals. God and man are not equal! Although the traditional sacrificial rites which besought the favour of God may have indicated hints of covenant, these rites were fundamentally concerned with divine appeasement.

These traditional sacrificial experiences are not synonymous with Biblical covenant. The Biblical God of the Covenant challenges tribal mores in personal encounter. God takes the initiative. He invites mankind to become his co-creator, his sons and daughters. Biblical covenant is concerned with the creation of a new redeemed peoplehood. Covenant in this context is about the redemptive recreation of fallen people, a recreation of fellowship between God and people. Repentance is required. These themes are hardly present in traditional concepts.

Nevertheless, there are some continuities between the African and Biblical heritage, as for example, reconciliation and cleansing is a prerequisite for acceptable sacrifice. Israel's cleansing preparations for God's encounter with them at Mount Sinai are somewhat similar to the peace preparations of the Gikuyu as they approached *Ngai* or the Acholi festival at the cave of a *Jok*.

Peace and covenant, the two are merged in African religion. The Bible says, God is love. Probably most traditional African societies would agree with the Gikuyu of Kenya, the Nuer of Sudan, or the Yoruba of Nigeria, whose respective perceptions of God we have described in some detail in the first chapter. For these peoples, God is the giver of peace. Just as the renewal sacrifices in the presence of God are rooted in peace, so also all the covenant themes within the African experience are affirmations of peace. Furthermore, covenant peace is anchored in justice. Doubtlessly this is true because the God who gives peace is also the One who is just.[13]

Next, we describe several covenant practices which are specifically concerned with person to person and community relationships.

Friendship Covenant

A covenant of friendship gives permanence to a precious relationship. Among the Abaluhya the covenant was consummated in the presence of elders who were witnesses. The covenanters would promise one another everlasting friendship, and then sacrifice a perfectly white chicken which they would roast and eat together. Eating the sacrificial bird in the presence of witnesses solemnized the covenant.[14]

Blood Brotherhood Covenant

The covenant of brotherhood is a further development of the covenant of friendship. A simple form of the brotherhood covenant involved sharing one another's blood. A typical method involved calling witnesses to join the prospective brothers on a certain day. The participants would make a solemn pledge to become brothers forever, and then would make a small incision on their forearms, and each would lick the other's blood. Sharing in each other's blood established a permanent relationship.[15]

Sometimes a brotherhood covenant would be initiated between two adversaries. Taking another example from the Abaluhya, the clan elders would sometimes insist on the establishment of a brotherhood covenant between two perpetual adversaries in order to bring peace between them. The adversaries would be brought before the clan elders and reprimanded for their disturbing hostilities, the factors contributing to the hostility would be confessed, and appropriate suggestions made as to how to live peacefully. After beating the adversaries, the elders would take a hen and strike them each with the hen. The hen was then slaughtered, the blood flowed over the sacrificial stones, and then the flesh was roasted and eaten by the covenanters. The participants would swear in the presence of the elders to live peacefully as brothers forever. Such a covenant could never be broken because the sacrificial blood had flowed over the stones of sacrifice in the ground uniting in covenant the living participants and the ancestral living-dead. Through the sacrificial hen the living-dead and the living had been irrevocably united in a sacred oath to live in peace as brothers. Should the covenant ever be broken, the living-dead would take vengeance.[16]

Variations of the blood brotherhood covenant are found throughout Africa. Very often blood brothers are created to bring inter-clan harmony. Chiefs of opposing clans may become blood brothers, thereby uniting their respective clans. Sometimes a colonial leader was invited to become a blood brother with an African chief. One of the most tragic stories known in East Africa was when the British Captain Lugard went through the blood brotherhood ceremony with the Gikuyu elder Waiyaki. Soon the Gikuyu became disturbed that Lugard and his fellow white men did not act like brothers towards the Africans. When Waiyaki tried to reprimand his blood brother, the astonishing response was arrest of Waiyaki and deportation. He died in transit to the coast. Tragically, Europeans did not have any idea of the meaning of brotherhood, at least not as understood by Africans.[17]

Kinship Covenant

The brotherhood covenant is similar to the re-establishment of kinship relationships through covenant. The kinship covenant was involved when things fell apart within the family. This covenant recreated harmony where family relationships had broken down. Approaches to the kinship covenant varied somewhat from society to society. Two examples suffice, again from the Bantu Abaluhya.

If family quarrels led to division, the whole society became involved, for divisiveness among the living not only affected social harmony, but also agitated the living-dead. The malevolence opened the doors for witchcraft, sorcery and other forms of evil. Consequently, clan elders did what they could to encourage reconciliation. When the family was ready for reconciliation, a day was set when all members of the extended family would meet in the home of the oldest family elder. Much reconciliatory preparation had preceded this eventful day. The day itself was a celebration that the process of reconciliation had been successful. Now all gathered together to sacrifice a sheep as a propitiation in the presence of the aggrieved living-dead. The sheep was disembowelled, and then each family member leaped across the intestines. In that leap they symbolically jumped from hostility into peace. In the presence of the living-dead, who were united with the living through the sacrificial blood which had been shed on the ground, they swore to live peacefully forever. The peace was affirmed by feasting together, the men together, and the women and children together. The feast was climaxed by beer drinking, with libations appropriately poured on behalf of the living-dead who were also present participating in the peace festival.[18]

Another form of the kinship covenant is reconciliation between a father and his son. If a son left the family homestead in anger and moved to another vicinity, or if he acted disrespectfully towards his father, reconciliation had to be effectuated. Neither the living nor the living-dead could remain silent when the most vital of all human relationships had been fractured, that is the fellowship between a father and his son. This is the link through which life flows. The rupture of the father-son relationship is death.

Consequently the clan elders intervened. They would go to see the son in order to persuade him to return to his father. If persuasion failed, they would command him to return and set a day for the reconciliation. On the set day they would personally escort the son, by force if need be, into his father's homestead. A feast of goat and chicken was prepared. The elders feasted together with the father and son and sipped from the common beer pot. In this ceremony father and son ate from the same dish and drank from the same pot; they ate together in the presence of the elders and the living-dead. Now they could not continue their hostility. Peace had been renewed; life had been restored . [19]

Adoption

One of the most remarkable forms of covenant in the African experience is adoption. African societies have enormous respect for the stranger. Hospitality for the stranger is boundless; the stranger is a blessing. The covenant of adoption is an extension of ordinary African hospitality so as to embrace the stranger totally. Through-adoption the stranger becomes a family member. Adoption is also applied to wider associations. A stranger clan can be adopted and fused into the clan structure of the host clan. Whatever the case may be, the purpose of adoption is to provide a way for the long term guest to become a permanent member of the family. Theologically, adoption is also right because all people are created by God, and therefore all are human. Adoption accents the true humanity of all;

even the guest and the stranger are people whom we need to accept fully and joyously.

Among the Meru of Kenya the adoption ceremony was called *kujiarwa na mburi,* meaning to be born with a goat. Women were never adopted because they became clan family members through marriage. The ceremony was only for males. The elder who wished to adopt a stranger as his son would teach the young man all the customs of the society. After he was confident that the newcomer was prepared to shoulder full responsibilities as a clan and family member, a day was appointed for the adoption ceremony. The prospective son had to provide three pots of honey beer and at least seven goats. One had to be spotless for the sacrificial oath of the covenant.

On the appointed day, the elders of the clan congregated, and select elders killed the sacrificial goat. Some of the blood was sprinkled on the head of the new son and father, and some was also sipped by the two. The blood spilled on the ground united the ancestral living-dead with the participants, and the rest of the blood was mixed with the cooked flesh which all the elders ate. In this manner the sacrificial blood united all the participants: the father and the new son, the living-dead, and the living clan. During the ceremony the elders commanded the new son to obey the laws of his adopted society, and they pronounced him a true son of the Meru people. The symbols of adoption were then awarded: a machete and a sword. The first was for farming. The latter was for the defence of the clan.

The covenant ceremony was concluded with feasting on the goats which the new son had contributed. The day was climaxed by communal beer drinking. The new son was blessed by the elders by spitting on his forehead. At evening the new son was welcomed into his new home by the sons of his new father. The evening was climaxed by feasting on food prepared by his new mother.[20]

Among the Gikuyu also, the covenant of adoption is a respected tradition. Dispossessed individuals or even whole families frequently migrated into Gikuyu territory and became serfs to Gikuyu landowners. The Bantu respect for human dignity could not tolerate indefinite servitude. Nevertheless, a period of time for testing the character and motives of the stranger was necessary before adoption could happen. If the stranger proved to be trustworthy, inevitably the day would come when the elder with whom the stranger lived would announce to the community that the time had come for him to give birth to a son. Elders were invited to participate, the principal elders being those most closely associated with the nearby shrine at the sacred *mugumo* tree. A bull was sacrificially slain, the elder father, first wife, and new son faced Mount Kenya and prayed for the blessing of *Ngai* on the newborn son and his parents. The elders also participated in the prayer of blessing.

The covenant was sealed when a true son of the adoptive household stepped forward to symbolize that he welcomed the new son to become his brother. The two men faced one another and, sitting on the hide of the slain animal, placed their hands together while the elders slipped a ring of skin from the slain bull over their joined hands thus uniting them symbolically through the sacrificial animal. The father pronounced a blessing to this effect: 'From today henceforth you have become my son by blood. From today you are brother to that man. My kinsmen, I will be responslile for this man. If he kills, I will be responsible. Likewise if someone kills him, the killer will pay me a hundred goats. This, my adopted son, has a right to my inheritance just as my son by birth.'

After the father's pronouncement of sonship, an elder mother stepped forward to cut their hands free from the bull hide rings, saying that she was cutting them loose to become separated, just as a mother gives birth to twins who then become separated, but who always remain twins. Still sitting in the symbolic womb of the moist bull hide, the two sons ate the heart of the sacrificial bull together. The women ululated just as was done when a male child was born. The participants feasted and rejoiced. The day was concluded by sharing in the communal drinking of beer.[21]

As far as I am aware, the participants are united through the slaying of a sacrificial animal in all covenants of adoption. These covenants are an affirmation of the inappropriateness of being a stranger forever. God has no place for second-class citizens. Through the covenant of adoption, the stranger becomes a son. He is welcomed into the new home by the true son and becomes his brother forever. He is a twice born man.[22]

The Marriage Covenant

In most African societies marriage is a covenant. In spite of polygamy being generally condoned in traditional African society, the marriage bond is enforced by covenant. There is a profound religious basis for marriage, which contradicts the view often held among scholars that traditional African marriage is a contract rather than a commitment. In past African societies, neither the monogamous nor the polygamous marriage could end unless the community itself sanctioned the divorce, which strongly hints at marriage as more of a covenant than a contract.

Among the Nandi of the Kalenjin cluster of societies in Kenya, the cows, sheep and goats offered by the prospective groom to the family of the bride are symbols of celebration and value. Marriage is for the continuation of the celebration of life; through marriage progeny are assured who perpetuate life. Animals offered as dowry for the bride are symbols of thanksgiving. And just as animals are for feasting, for sustenance, for nourishment, for joy, for living in ordinary Nandi life, so do they become symbols of life and celebration when they are formally transferred to the bride's family after the marriage is solemnized.

The ceremony takes place in the homestead of the groom. Both groups of relatives take part in drinking the ceremonial beer as a sacrament of unity. Milk is also shared in sacramental drinking, after which there is feasting together, in fellowship and union. The symbols of marriage are then exchanged; the bride and groom placed on each other's wrists special grass bracelets. They are then blessed by the elders who anoint them with a special sacred oil mixed with a bit of saliva. All of this takes place during the wedding night. The following day there is feasting and dancing.

Confession completes the wedding ceremony. Both families sit and discuss the wedding to discover if there has been any slight or inhospitality. Guests who feel they have not been properly respected are invited to express their grievances. If the bride's family is unhappy that the groom's family has not provided for them adequately, apologies are made. Forgiveness is extended and accepted. All grievances have to be expressed and resolved through confession and forgiveness before people return to their homes. 'Clean inside' is essential to future harmonious inter-family relationships. These are the firm bases for marriage among the Nandi, but change among them, as elsewhere in Africa, has taken place quite often to the detriment of marriage as it was practised in the past.

The grass bracelets were a sign of the marriage covenant. Among the Kalenjin Kipsigis the ceremony of exchanging bracelets could never be performed again for a woman after her first marriage. Even if she became a widow, the first bracelet ceremony was binding; although she might 'marry' again, the bracelet ceremony was not repeated and children born through her second marriage belonged to her first husband even though he was not living. [23] This was typical of many African societies. All the children born to a woman belonged to her first husband; she remained his wife forever. In some societies even a 'divorced' woman was buried at the homestead of her first husband.

In most African societies animal sacrifices seal the marriage covenant. J.W.J. Mwangi, writing in memory of her beloved grandmother, recalls the traditional marriage covenant among the Gikuyu. When a Gikuyu boy wished to propose to a girl his parents visited the home of the prospective bride to inquire formally about her willingness to marry their son. If she consented, she took a horn of beer, and after sipping it herself, passed it to her parents, and then to the parents of the young man. The communal sipping of beer became the first symbol of covenant.

The formalization of the engagement involved close relatives and friends. Beer was shared and prayers offered to *Ngai*. These encounters might continue for some time while the dowry arrangements were being worked out. Trust and harmonious relationships had to be established between the two families. Finally the families were ready for sealing the engagement through the pouring of the blood of unity, at which time the engaged couple were purified by the sacrificial slaughter of one sheep of only one colour, black, white, or brown. The blood and stomach contents were sprinkled on the homestead gateway facing Mount Kenya, signifying the desire of the couple to be purified and blessed by *Ngai*. The families feasted together nearby eating the roasted flesh of rams. The two clans were thus symbolically united in covenant by God and the living-dead, who had received the sacrificial blood.

The marriage was solemnized with a great feast. Six fat rams were sacrificially slaughtered. The bride herself assisted in slaying the first sheep and she was given the kidneys to eat. This was a sign that she affirmed the marriage and that she would never break the marriage covenant. The elders assisting in the sacrifice also symbolized the presence of God and the living-dead in the sealing of the marriage. The sacrificial blood and the eating of the sacrificed animals together bound the families and the couple together in covenant. All had been sealed together by the covenantal blood: the living-dead, the elders who were the closest to God and the living-dead, the clan heads, the families, and the bridal pair.

After the marriage sacrifice, the bride could begin to work with her mother-in-law in the fields, but she remained in her home, until the day for the consummation of the marriage. On that day she was surprised and 'kidnapped' by friends of the groom, who seized her while she was at work, and ran with her screaming and kicking to the house of the groom's mother where she stayed until her own house was built. As she was carried along, well-wishers pronounced blessing on her. After eight days of honeymoon, a fat sheep was slaughtered and she was anointed with its oil as a sign of blessing and adoption into the new family.

After several days, she returned once more to her parent's home for special blessings. Sometimes another sheep was slaughtered, and prayers were offered asking for forgiveness for any wrong which she might have done since childhood, which would prevent the blessing of God on the marriage. She was blessed by her parents by anointing with oil. She had brought a gourd of beer along for this ceremony, and all sipped from the gourd together as a sign of communion and forgiveness. She then returned to her new home with a free conscience, assured that her childhood naughtiness was forgiven and forgotten. She returned to her new home laden with presents to warm the bridal house.[24]

If marriage is a covenant in the African heritage, then it is not surprising that covenant devices are also employed when a marriage runs into trouble. The degree to which covenant symbols are brought to bear on the marriage reconciliation process depends on the seriousness of the rupture. Several examples will illustrate covenant renewal in marriage.

Carren Omwenga describes marriage covenant renewal among her people, the Kisii. If a wife had been adulterous or had left her husband for an extended period of time, her family would attempt to arrange a reconciliation. On a predetermined day she was taken from her parents' home to her husband's home with a goat, which was provided by her father. She was only allowed to enter the husband's homestead if she was accompanied by this goat as well as a few people (family members including her parents) from her home, who served as witnesses to the reconciliation.

Having arrived at the husband's home, she was not allowed to go straight to her house, but went to her mother-in-law's house with the goat that accompanied her. Here the covenant was made, witnessed by the few people who had accompanied the estranged woman and also some neighbours of the husband.

The woman was made to sit on one side (left) of the house and the man also sat on the opposite side, facing each other. An elder from the man's home then placed the goat which the woman brought from her home in between them and slaughtered it there. He then called the two of them . . . and dipped both their hands in the blood of the goat and . . . put them together. After this they crossed and went to each other's side and then came together and sat on one side . . . joined together once more as a couple by the blood of the goat. The elder who dipped both their hands in the blood witnessed their coming together and the oath they took that they would never divorce again.[25]

The goat was then roasted and the participants ate together, thereby consummating the covenant through communal eating of the sacrificial goat. Normally this kind of sacrifice signified the need for major atonement because of a serious breakdown in the marriage, as in such cases as adultery or prolonged separation and unfaithfulness.

Among the Abaluhya, sacrifice was also offered for marriage reconciliation. If a couple separated, private attempts at reconciliation were initiated. If these efforts failed, then kinsmen and elders were asked to come on a set day, probably to the home of the wife, to help bring reconciliation. The couple were invited to share everything, for only in that way could peace be restored. First the husband would speak, and then the wife. Hidden hostilities had to be vented, or healing could not take place. They were encouraged to say everything without shyness. After the issues were thoroughly understood, the elders would give counsel, often through the use of wisdom questions: Woman, did you not decide to marry this man of your own free choice? Man, do you not know that your wife is not a cow to be beaten? Do you not realize that your separation is not in accord with the customs of our society? They would give counsel. If the counsel was accepted, reconciliation was effectuated.

Normally the husband then left his wife's home, and after several days she would return to her husband's house accompanied by at least one kinsman. She would come with flour, meat, and a chicken. The chicken was slain by her brother-in-law, a meal was prepared, and the husband and his kinsmen joined her in the house for the meal. After eating together, they poured a libation of water on the floor. The libation propitiated the living-dead and united them in a covenant of reconciliation. On the other hand, the slain chicken was a sacrifice for forgiveness, and the meal together represented the renewal of fellowship in the presence of the kinsmen and the living-dead.[26]

However, if the breach in relationships was very serious, if the wife left under oath never to return, then the elders accepted with equal seriousness the duty to effectuate cleansing of the ill will and the recreation of the marriage. In that case the elders and families would meet on a particular day for a sacrifice of reconciliation. The guilty party would provide a perfect sheep of one colour. An elder would slaughter the sheep sacrificially. The blood flowed into the ground uniting the ancestral living-dead in the covenant of renewal. The couple stepped in the dung of the sheep and dung was also scattered here and there as a sign that the evil which had entered the home was to be cleansed and thrown away. The assembly ate the roasted flesh of the sacrificed sheep in a communion of reconciliation. When the families and the couple had eaten together, that was a sign that peace had returned. Harmony had been restored. It was a solemn occasion. There was no dancing.[27]

We have looked at only a few examples of marriage as covenant, and covenantal aspects of renewal of disrupted marriage. All African societies have devices for helping an estranged couple become reconciled. Confession and counsel are integral to all these reconciliation systems. Even contractual marriages participate in counsel when things fall apart. Nevertheless, in most societies there is an added reinforcement to reconciliation.

This is the covenant dimension in which deity, the living-dead, the elders, the clan, the families, and the couple are united together in a covenant of reconciliation through the sacrificial blood of a perfect animal or fowl, usually an animal or bird in the prime of life which is of one colour. The efficacy of the sacrifice is affirmed by communal beer drinking as a sign of peace. The covenant of reconciliation is the covenant of peace.

Land Covenants

In agrarian African societies land is a sacred trust. In pastoral societies the animal which gives sustenance is valued as God's good gift to the people, but in sedentary societies it is the land which is especially sacred. Earlier we had mentioned that the Gikuyu myth of origin includes a myth about land; God gave them the land as their heritage, He is the Divider of the Land.

LAND TRANSFERS AMONG THE GIKUYU
Since land was a sacred gift from God as well as a gift of nature, the Gikuyu resisted selling their land as much as possible in the past. Similarly, Gikuyu land purchases were never in perpetuity and could

be made permanent only through such social binding mechanisms as blood brotherhood or adoption of the selling family into Gikuyu society. Similar adoption procedures were carried out whenever a Gikuyu was involved in any transfer of land with non-Gikuyu societies as was done when adopting an individual outsider into a Gikuyu home. The Gikuyu purchaser would arrange with his parents to adopt as brother the man whose land he desired, and in this way the land would be transferred to the family. Land transfers among brothers were acceptable; God had given the land to the Gikuyu people as a whole. The theological problem developed only when land was transferred from one society to another.

However, in spite of land transfers within the Gikuyu society not needing adoption as such, other forms of covenant pertaining to land were practised, in such cases as disputes over boundaries or the sale of land. Among the Gikuyu, especially, God participated in the land covenant, because he is the one who is the Divider of Land.

The procedure for land sale involving only Gikuyu parties was quite elaborate. After the Gikuyu owner and his fellow Gikuyu buyer had agreed on the price, they called several elders to join them in consummating the agreement. The elders queried under oath whether the land really did belong to the seller. They also made certain that the price was mutually agreed. Then a red goat was slaughtered sacrificially. The leading elder took the stomach and entrails and followed the two men involved in the transaction around the plot of land scattering bits of the entrails along the boundary. Trees and flowers were then planted also along the boundary. In this manner the boundary acquired covenantal permanence. Then the elders and the two men sat in the middle of the field, and two small rings were made of the skin of the red goat and placed on the right hand of each of the two men. This was a sign that, through the land transaction, they had become brothers. The goat was then roasted and eaten communally. Usually beer was drunk and libations poured, thereby inviting the ancestral living-dead to affirm and participate in the ceremony. The agreement was reinforced by fear; anyone who tampered with the boundary was cursed. If later on a tree did blow down along the boundary, or a flood washed the markers away, the elders were invited to help the two neighbours replant the tree and remark the boundary. The boundary was spiritually and communally sanctioned.[28]

LAND DISPUTES AMONG THE MERU

Among the Meru, who live on the eastern slopes of Mount Kenya, land disputes were settled through reconciliation and sacrifice. The two disputants called the clan elders into council to settle the matter. Claims and counter claims were heard, and a decision made which the two litigants were required to accept. Then the litigants brought a goat. As the goat was slain, the litigants would both take hold of a knot of grass, and an elder would take blood from the goat and sprinkle it on their hands and on the grass knot saying that they were now cleansed of the ill will which had been tied into the grass knot. The cleansed men then threw the knot of grass into the sacrificial fire, symbolizing that the evil was removed and burned. All their jealousies and malice had been cleansed by the blood and consumed by the fire. The goat was roasted, and the assembly ate the sacrificial goat, and participated in communal beer drinking. Libations were poured for the living-dead. The eating and drinking together was a sign of renewed communion.

Peace had been restored, but the peace was reinforced by fear. If the litigants ever again renewed their enmity, they would die just as the goat had died. Death was the consequence of breaking the covenant of peace. Malice brought death. It had to be permanently eradicated.[29]

Peace Covenants Following Warfare

Warfare epitomizes the breakdown of harmony. The violence of warfare is disharmony gone mad. It is the opposite of peace, which is the will of God and of the ancestral living-dead. If nearness to God is peace, then the breakdown of peace in warfare is certainly a form of distance from God. Consequently, there is probably no dimension of African thought and practice which is more profound than the covenants of peace following warfare. This matter is so important that we shall comment briefly on the techniques and theological undergirding of several societies in East Africa in their efforts for regaining peace after warfare.

Among the Samburu, inter-clan feuds frequently developed over competition concerning girls by the young men. To end the feud or violence, the leaders would initiate a peace parley. All the young men were required to present themselves. The issues were discussed, and then the elders offered green (for peace) or dry (for no peace) twigs to the youth. If the youth accepted the offer of peace, they each selected a green twig. If any youth selected a dry twig, it was obvious that the parley had not been wholly successful. Community pressure normally succeeded in getting all to accept the peace. Then a white bull, as a sign of peace, was killed, and the skin of the bull was carved into strips, which were tied around the arms of the young men, thus showing that through the sacrifice of the white peace bull, they were bound by covenant to live in peace. No youth with the white bull's skin peace bracelet dared to fight with his clansmen again. The peace assembly was completed with the elders feasting on the bull's meat together. The youth dispersed to their homesteads and ate a lesser feast together. The act of eating together consummated the covenant of peace.

In case of war with a non-Samburu society, e.g. the Maasai or Boran, the elders of the respective societies met to discuss the unfortunate eruption of violence. They jointly called a peace parley, which required the presence of all the young warriors of the respective societies. The formalities included the breaking of a spear by selected elders from each side. Then the two ends of the broken weapon were speared into the ground upright, apart from each other. All the elders went past the broken spear shafts symbolizing that the broken weapon had become the gate of peace.

After they went past the gate of peace, each side took honey and smeared it with their own hands on the lips of those in the other side. Honey symbolizes the sweetness of peace. By placing honey on the lips of one's former enemies, one showed that both societies were once more at peace.

The covenant was concluded by killing a white bull. The now-united societies roasted and ate the sacrificial animal together, pronouncing anathemas on anyone who ever again disturbed the peace. Blessing was proclaimed on all peacemakers. The act of eating the sacrificial peace bull together solidified the peace covenant.[30]

A friend has told of a particular recent incident involving the Samburu. In 1977 violence exploded between the Samburu and the Meru over a misunderstanding concerning the sale of a cow. Leaders from both sides acted quickly to forestall hostilities by convening a council of peace. A sheep of only one colour was slain and its blood sprinkled over the entire assembly. In this manner the potential for escalating violence was quickly nipped in the bud.

The Abaluhya had a similar practice. If war broke out between them and a neighbouring society, the elders on both sides called a peace council. The antagonists formed two semicircles facing one another. All their weapons were stuck in the ground between them. Under the leadership of a diviner, the causes of the war were thoroughly discussed. Thereafter, the conflicting parties agreed on the appropriate steps to end the conflict. Forms of restitution were arranged; if cattle were stolen, they were to be returned in full, unless the raiders were hungry. Then an animal was sacrificed. Very often a black peace dog was slain in sacrifice. A leading elder from the side which had been "victorious" in the battle would hold the head end of the live dog, and an elder from the defeated side would grasp the hind part. Then the dog was slain by cutting it in half. After the sacrifice of the dog, the participants stood in the blood of the slain animal. Then they ate together and drank ceremonial beer. They poured libations for the living-dead, beseeching them to bless the covenant of peace, and besought God to witness the covenant. Dancing and festivity followed. Usually the peace was consummated by arranging several inter-societal marriages.

In some situations the Abaluhya preferred to sacrifice a goat or a sheep. Some of the blood was poured out in sacrifice, and some of it was drunk by the elders. This was a powerful symbol of unity. The blood spilled on the ground had united the living-dead of both sides.

The living were similarly united by drinking the blood of the slain animal. This covenant of peace was powerfully reinforced by fear. If anyone broke the covenant of unity and peace, they would be cursed by the living, the living-dead and God.[31]

The nearby Nilotic Luo participated in a variation of the Abaluhya peace covenant. A Luo friend told of a covenant-making ceremony between his people and the Maasai. The elders arranged for peace parleys, and after both sides had agreed on the need and satisfactory terms for the peace, a great inter-societal rally was convened on the border where the battles had been fought. Men, women, youth and children convened along the border on the covenant day. They chopped down trees whose white sap is used as poison for arrow tips. These poison trees were formed into a fence along the common border, with the antagonists facing one another across the newly formed poison-tree fence. The weapons of warfare were placed along the fence—spears, bows and arrows, swords and shields. This fence of poison wood and weapons was a symbol of the war which had divided the two communities.

Then they took a black dog and laid it across the fence. The dog was cut into two and blood was allowed to flow through the fence and on to the ground, on both sides of the fence. Then the mothers with suckling babies exchanged their young back and forth across the fence so that Maasai mothers could suckle Luo babies and Luo mothers suckle Maasai babies. This was followed by prayers, the respective elders beseeching God to bless the covenant of peace. The participants pronounced anathemas on any one who ever crossed that fence to do evil.

The covenant had united the two sides in a bond of peace. The dog, which in this case symbolized evil, had been slain. The evil of the societies, as it were, had been vicariously cleansed through the sacrificial death of the dog. The blood had transformed the war barrier into a sign of peace. The warring parties had become brothers by suckling one another's babies.

Towards the end of the last century the pastoral Kipsigis and the agrarian Kisii had perpetual border conflict. Repeated efforts were made to establish peace through covenant. On many occasions the elders met with the warriors to arrange peace. After grievances were confessed and appropriate steps towards restitution processed, both sides poured libations of beer on behalf of the living-dead, who were requested to be present for the covenant-making. Sacrifice was offered of a white goat, a bull and a black cock. The sacrificial blood flowed into the earth, uniting the aggrieved living-dead in a covenant of peace. The flesh of the animals and the ceremonial beer was drunk commonly. When thus united, the war was supposed to cease forever.

In this case the wars stopped only temporarily. As soon as a new set of age-mates achieved warrior status, the hostilities started again. The peacemaking process was renewed repeatedly by the elders, only to collapse again within several years' time.

Contemporary residents of the area say that it is only through the Church that these traditionally hostile communities have finally been united in a covenant of peace.[32] We shall comment more on that perception later. To what extent can or does the Church fulfil the peace covenant of traditional African societies?

Were the Covenants Adequate?

This survey of covenant practices in Africa does indicate that the quest for peace is one of the deepest felt needs among African peoples. This is not surprising, for peace is a prominent theme in all the religions of mankind. Nevertheless, this is a study of religion and faith in Africa, and peace is the paramount concern. Yet there were no illusions concerning the formidable obstacles to peace. An awareness of the nature of the obstacles to peace calls for an equally serious response. The covenant, in all its varied forms, is one of the most serious and profound expressions of the quest for peace. Was it adequate?

Recently I asked my Tanzanian bishop that question. His response was, 'No'. He went on to say, 'We tried hard to capture peace, to live in peace, but we were not successful.'

As evidence of failure I thought he would point to the fortifications which are still seen on many hills in his community, where the warriors used to congregate for attacks on neighbouring societies.

But he did not. Instead he went on to say, 'The most serious dimension of our failure was evident in witchcraft. In my boyhood days witchcraft was a plague. We really did not know how to forgive deeply enough to prevent witches from developing right from within our communities. Unforgiving people became witches. It was a fearsome thing, which nearly destroyed us.'

And then with quiet sobriety he continued, 'I am thankful for the Gospel, because through the Gospel I have experienced forgiveness, and I have been made free to forgive. Otherwise I too could become an evil person, a witch whose presence is a curse rather than a blessing. How I thank God that through Jesus I am a forgiven person!'

Is my bishop right? It is not the purpose of this study to investigate that question, although it is true that a multitude of first generation African Christians share a similar witness of having found joy and fulfilment in their quest for peace in Jesus Christ, a fulfilment of peace which they sought for, but were never able to satisfactorily achieve through the traditional covenant systems. In Biblical terms one would say that the traditional sacrificial or covenantal system could not adequately deal with human sinfulness. (See Hebrews 9:13, 14.)

At a more pragmatic level, the traditional mechanisms for achieving peace are in serious disarray in our modern times. A Turkana elder in northern Kenya said it very well recently, at a meeting with a Church delegation who were discussing the problem of reconciliation between some clans who were engaged in hostilities. He said, 'When I was a child, our elders knew how to become reconciled. They had ways to establish peace among themselves. Now all that has changed. The old methods do not work any more.'

This Turkana sage is only partly right. Certainly there is a deep wealth of insight within the traditional heritage which is universally valid. It is regrettable when modernity creeps across a society like a glacial movement, destroying all that has been previously present. That is utterly dehumanizing. Responsible progress must tap deeply into the heritage of the past; authentic progress draws from treasures. both 'old and new'. (Matthew 13:52.)

One of the most serious challenges to the traditional covenant mechanisms is the expansion in scale which all societies in modern Africa are experiencing. Traditional techniques were tailored within a homogeneous group. Modern nationhood and pan-African as well as universal world relationships impinge upon the integrity of the small-scale community. Traditional peacemaking techniques become almost impotent in a situation of massive mobility and scale expansion with consequential cultural interchange not only with neighbouring societies, but with foreigners. The traditional techniques were never intended to cope with societies in the process of such expansion. This is one reason why many of the traditional covenant mechanisms have collapsed and died out.

Nevertheless, traditional themes have penetrated the modern experience and persisted. This is especially true in the Church. The Church is a community of faith, which is theologically attuned to many of the insights and aspirations revealed in the traditional covenant experience. In fact, many Christians in Africa believe that the Gospel is a marvellous fulfilment of the quest for peace which is so explicitly developed in the traditional religion. Only recently a mature African churchman, who is also a first-generation Christian, told me, 'The sacrificial system and the covenants of African traditional religion are very similar to the Old Testament. Just as the Old Testament helped the early Church to understand Christ, so our traditional religion has helped us to understand and accept the Gospel.'

A Gospel which fulfils both transforms and preserves that which it fulfils. Although cultures may be insensitive and destructive as they collide and interact with one another, the Gospel is never so. As the fulfiller of the quest for peace, the Gospel also preserves and nourishes that quest. It is for this reason that Christianity in Africa has developed more and different interpretations of the Gospel than are to be found in non-African Christian communities. In the next chapter we shall describe some of those perceptions. However, first we need to summarize some of the main covenant themes which we have discussed above.

70

Covenant Themes

This survey of covenant practices in the African experience reveals common themes which appear repeatedly.

First, covenants establish relationships which are different from kinship ties. When the deepest level of kinship links are strained, a covenant can recreate the broken ties. Through covenant, human fellowship and relationships are ontologically established.

Second, a covenant is a very serious and profound matter. Making one is not lightly undertaken. It affects the entire community and is witnessed and endorsed by the community, the living-dead, and often by God as well. The covenant is everlasting. To break a covenant is to invite a curse. Although covenant is life-enhancing at the profoundest level of ontocracy, it is also death-enhancing when broken.

Third, the covenant attempts to affirm and recreate the person's original ontocratic unity with God and humanity. It is a quest for and a sign of the primal harmony of life and community. It is an attempt to recreate and sustain life-enhancing harmony.

Fourth, the covenant can be established only when there is openness and transparency. Confession is a central aspect of all covenants which are instituted to bring peace when relationships have broken down. Even in the more joyous events such as marriage, transparency themes are often evident. Within the covenant experience there is a recognition that candour, confession, and forgiveness are essential to good human relationships.

Fifth, covenants which are sought because of a breakdown in relationships often require restitution before the covenant can be established. Even in covenants which are not necessarily reconciliatory, there is usually some form of gift exchange. These gifts may be for penance or gratitude. Whatever the case, the purpose of the gifts is to affirm personhood. The wrongdoer relieves his guilt by giving a gift, and the aggrieved feels affirmed in the receiving of the gift; the bride is affirmed by the bride price, and the groom is pleased by the bride. Balance and person affirmation are central to all forms of covenant.

Sixth, covenants require sacrifice. In some covenants the participants shed their own blood and exchange some blood in the covenant ceremony. In others an animal is sacrificed. So far as I am aware, all African covenants require some form of sacrificial shedding of blood. The blood is essential because life is in the blood; covenants are for the preservation of life through the solidifying of the community. Sacrificial blood is the seal of the covenant.

Seventh, the covenant is celebrated by feasting together, usually on the roasted flesh of the sacrificial animal. The eating is a communion, a celebration of life in a community. Thus the covenant might be profound, serious, or even sombre, yet it is also a joyous, life affirming fellowship and feasting.

Finally, the covenant is affirmed by the community, by the elders, by the living-dead, and often times also by God. The whole community is blessed by witnessing the covenant, and in turn the covenanters are affirmed by the entire ontocratic community of life.

What are the practical and theological implications of the African experience of Covenant for the Christian Church? To what extent do the traditional African understandings have implications for Christian understandings of community, of Church, of reconciliation, of peace and justice, of humanity? What is the nature of a Christian theology of reconciliation in the context of African Covenant themes? We turn to those questions in the following chapter.

COVENANTS FOR JUSTICE, RECONCILIATION AND PEACE

REFERENCES

1. E. Bolaji Idowu, *African Traditional Religion, A Definition,* London, S.C.M., 1973, 149-65.
2. E. Bolaji Idowu, *Olodumare, God in Yoruba Belief,* London, Longman, 1962. 140-43, 144-68: (Note: Idowu's study represents a very perceptive case-study of the moral-religious dimensions of God-man relationships in Yoruba society, and the covenantal aspects of the cult of Olodumare.)
3. Jomo Kenyatta, *Facing Mount Kenya,* London, 1938, reprinted by Mercury Books, 1961, 1-4.
4. Samuel G. Kibicho, *The Kikuyu Conception of God,* Ph.D. Dissertation, Nashville, Vanderbilt University, 1972, 21.
5. Kenyatta, op. cit., 244-52.
6. Ibid., 247.
7. Ibid., 249-52.
8. Okot p'Bitek, *Religion of the Central Luo,* Nairobi, E.A.L.B., 1971, 68, 72, 73, 80-85.
9. Ibid., 85.
10. Evans Pritchard, *Nuer Religion,* Oxford, O.U.P., 1956, 1, 49, 95, 106.
11. p'Bitek, op. cit., 69.
12. Ibid., 68-85.
13. Kibicho, op. cit., 39.
14. B.A. Mutoro, 'Covenant', K.U.C. archives, n.d., 9.
15. Caren Omwenga, 'A Comparative Study of Covenant in my Traditional Community and in the Old Testament', Nairobi, K.U.C. archives, n.d. 7.
16. Mutoro, op. cit., 9-11.
17. Kibicho, op. cit., 27, 28.
18. Mary Washika Were, 'Comparative Study of Covenant in the Abaluhya Community — The Wanga Sub Tribe — And in the Old Testament', Nairobi, K.U.C. archives, n.d., 7.
19. Ibid., 8.
20. E. M. Kamundi, 'A Comparative Study of Covenant in Meru Traditional Community and in the Old Testament', Nairobi, K.U.C. archives, n.d., 7,8.
21. Margaret Kamau, 'Attitudes Towards Strangers in the Traditional Society and Within the Church', Nairobi, K.U.C. archives, n.d., 8, 9.
22. Rhoda J. Keino, 'Covenant', Nairobi, K.U.C. archives, 1979.
23. Rosemary Chebet Milgo, 'Covenant', Nairobi, K.U.C. archives, n.d., 3, 4.
24. J.W.J. Mwangi, 'Covenant', Nairobi, K.U.C. Archives, n.d., 5-8 Kenyatta, *Facing Mount Kenya,* 163-174.
25. Omwenga, op. cit., 3,4.
26. Judith M. Wakala, 'A Comparative Study of Reconciliation Between a Husband and Wife in Traditional Abaluhya Society and Abaluhya Church Today', Nairobi, K.U.C. archives, 1979, 9-11.
27. Rosemary K.N. Musakali, 'Reconciliation Between a Man and His Wife', Nairobi, K.U.C. Archives, 1979, 5.
28. Mwangi, op. cit., 11-14.
29. Kamunde, op. cit., 8.

30. J.H. Wario, 'The Covenant', Nairobi, K.U.C. archives, n.d.
31. Gerald A. Okello, 'A Case Study of Reconciliation Between Warring Clans in Traditional Abaluhya Society, Within the Church, and also Within the Umma', Nairobi, K.U.C. archives, 1978.
32. Bathsheba K. Mareri, 'Reconciliation in Warring Clans', Nairobi, K.U.C. archives, n.d., 12,13.

PART TWO

Christian African Experience of
Justice, Reconciliation and Peace

A thirst
To have a thirst, a void which longs to be filled
You know nothing at all!
Have you read the little book they call the Gospel?
Have you settled down to read ten times over that little book
they call the Gospel?
Little man, do you know Jesus Christ?
Do you know that he is living and that he sees?
He sees you, he looks at you.
What will you do when you come across such a love as
you have never dreamed of welcoming?
Since the coming of Jesus Christ it is no longer difficult to love
nobly
We are born to die
We die in order to live
We are born, we live, we pass by
We live, as we pass by,
Passing by, we fashion our eternity.

Michel Kayoya

Chapter IV

THE GOSPEL OF RECONCILIATION

Makka was intensely angry. His only wife, Mirengeri, had become a Christian. Even a beating did not cure her of the new folly.

Mirengeri had problems too. She did not know how a Christian wife should behave towards her husband. So she brought her questions to the Church.

Should she make beer for her husband? The wise men and women of the congregation urged her to keep on making beer, for after all Makka was her husband.

Makka did not appreciate Mirengeri's singing around the homestead, and especially Christian songs. The Church urged her to sing only in her heart, and to avoid any needless irritation.

One Sunday Makka happened to walk by the whitewashed Church building at the time of Sunday worship. Just to rest a little, he sat under some nearby shade trees. He also listened as best as he could to bits of the worship service.

The next Sunday Makka happened to walk by again. This time he sat closer to the Church. Next Sunday he rested from his Sunday walk under the cool eaves of the Church building, right under a window. On another Sunday he sat in the doorway during the entire service, and finally he entered the building. Then one Sunday Makka stood during the Church service, asking those present to forgive him for his anger towards his wife and the Christian community. He asked the congregation to pray for him, for he also desired to become a Christian.

The congregation burst into song. Another person had returned to the loving Father; Makka had confessed faith in Jesus Christ; a man and his wife had become reconciled.

The story of Makka and Mirengeri is multiplied tens of thousands of times every week across the African continent. There is a Christward movement within Africa today which is unprecedented in the history of the Christian Church.

Theological Reflection

In the first part of this book we have reviewed approaches to justice, peace and reconciliation in the traditional African experience, a heritage which is rich and vibrant, a heritage whose spiritual and psychological insights are impressively astute. Yet we are now confronted by the fact that millions of Africans have grasped the Gospel of Jesus Christ with an enthusiasm which is unparalleled in the history of Christian mission. With 300,000,000 professing Christians, Africa is rapidly becoming predominantly Christian. The centre of gravity of Christian faith is gradually slipping southward; in our generation, the African Church is recovering momentum and leadership within the world Christian Church which it lost during the seventh century, as Islamic conquest gained ascendancy over the ancient churches of northern Africa. At the dawn of the twenty-first century, the modern resurgence of Christianity in Africa is a fact which is altering the theological and ecclesiastical profile of the world Christian community.[1]

The modern African Church is beginning to express her faith theologically. Previously the newly born African congregations have been primarily concerned with evangelism. For a century a principal concern throughout sub-Saharan Africa has been the evangelization of peoples. Across this vast continent African evangelists walked their feet sore taking the Gospel from village to village and from society to society; they formed churches wherever they went. Their mission of evangelism has been astonishingly fruitful. Currently there are about 8,000,000 baptisms per year. In some African societies today as many as 95 per cent of the populace are professing Christians. Church growth in many areas, still largely unevangelized, is roughly twice the rate of demographic increase.

With the evangelization of many sub-Saharan peoples rapidly nearing a sort of consummation, the Church is now entering a period of serious theological reflection. What does the Gospel mean in the African context? Obviously it means much; otherwise people would not believe it so enthusiastically. They would not give their lives for the Gospel if it were not perceived as a gift which supersedes all other values. What is there about the life, death and resurrection of Jesus Christ which is so precious? Why is Jesus attractive? Why is his Church growing? Why do the peoples sing and dance with joy in the name of Jesus? What is there within the African traditional heritage which 'prepares' the African peoples to understand and grasp the Gospel so enthusiastically?

Some may suggest that the African response to the Gospel is superficial, that it is merely another aspect of western colonization. This is hardly so. Encounter with the west can hardly be the fundamental ingredient. Other societies have had a much more prolonged and overwhelming encounter with western society than Africa, and yet have remained quite resistant to the evangelistic invitation of the Church. Why have the African peoples been receptive? Could it be that God in his providence had prepared African peoples to hear and believe the Gospel through the gift of their traditional religious heritage? Many African Christians believe that this is true: belief in one transcendent God, belief in the hereafter, the concept of a sad separation between God and humankind, the understanding of the person and his place in the universe, insights concerning sacrifice and powers, and many other aspects of the African heritage are probably the most important reason for African responsiveness to the Gospel. Within the African world view, the Gospel makes much sense and it comes through as being very good news indeed. This is one dimension to the theological reflection which is now developing in Africa.

Another theological dimension deals with the challenge of contextualising the Gospel. How does the Gospel fit most appropriately into the African context? What does it affirm and what does it judge in the African experience? How do the African perceptions of the Gospel make the new converts more sensitive to the theological and religious issues raised in the good news? What aspects of traditional theologies are enriched and expanded by the Gospel? What dimensions of traditional cosmologies are inappropriate for Christian belief and practice?

In recent decades the African Church has struggled with these questions. As African peoples approached independence after the colonial ordeal, the Christian communities felt the urgent need to interpret theologically what it means to be an African and a Christian.

Several expatriate church persons have tried to help the theological enterprise along. One thinks particularly of the Protestant contribution through the pen of John V. Taylor whose *The Primal Vision* stimulated fresh theological reflection, particularly with reference to the Church's attitude towards the living-dead.[2] The Catholics have also been prolific. The Gaba Pastoral Institute in Uganda has made a continental impact through the research and writing of scholars such as Fr. Aylward Shorter.[3] These and other studies undertaken by perceptive non-African churchpersons are complementary to reflective work by the Africans themselves.

During the past three decades there has been a flood of African scholarship related to African perceptions of the Gospel. Much of this contribution relates especially to definitions of the nature of African traditonal religion. Textbooks have been written for secondary schools and universities on the African traditional heritage. This stream of research and reflection continues with vigour and resiliency. There is a sense of urgency in these writings, a sense that the indigenization of the Gospel must include a serious understanding of African roots.

Nevertheless, the study of roots is not the only dimension to this African theological quest. Complementing the quest for an understanding of the meaning of Africanness, there has also been a search for a contextualization of the Gospel. African scholars have been contributing to this search. One of the pioneers has been Professor Harry Sawyerr of the University College, University of Sierra Leone.[4] Professor John S. Mbiti[5] of East Africa is an outstanding scholar who has written prolifically, although his studies generally accent the African heritage, whereas Professor Sawyerr concentrated much of his effort on the Biblical perspective. Other scholars of note are Professor Bolaji Idowu,[6] Dr. Byang Kato,[7] Professor Kwesi Dickson,[8] and Professor John S. Pobee.[9] The latter has written the fascinating book, *Toward an African Theology,* in which he carefully compares several key Biblical doctrines with African understandings. This book is a step forward in the quest for an

African Christian theology, because it uniquely combines an earnest commitment to Biblical faith with a sincere appreciation for the African heritage. Although one cannot mention all the noteworthy contributors to the quest for an African theology, others who readily come to mind include Fashole-Luke, Manas Buthelezi, Desmond Tutu, Alan Boesak, Charles Nyamiti, Bishop P.A. Kalilombe and Bishop F. Kivengere, Henry Okullu, Jesse Mugambi, Nicodemus Kirima, Jacob Olupona, Kwame Bediako. Christian theology which is both Biblical and African is being developed today; the process is fascinating.[10]

As a former university teacher of comparative religion, I am aware of the pitfalls involved in attempting to compare or synthesize two different faith systems. By way of example, some have suggested that the best way to interpret the sonship of Christ is to compare him with traditional chiefs in African systems in which a chief has divine attributes. This kind of comparison is dangerous. We know that even the apparent similarity between two faith systems is often not similar because each religious aspect is rooted in a whole world system of faith and values. Thus, although there are similarities, for example, between the Christian concept of covenant and that of the traditional African experience, we need to avoid equating the two, as there are apparent incompatibilities which make each one distinct from the other. For example, the role of the living-dead in many traditional covenant experiences is in some aspects quite incompatible with the Biblical theocentric covenant. Continuities and discontinuities, similarities and dissimilarities are present wherever the Gospel breaks in.

The web of inter-relationships which support a people's values is so intricately interwoven that we cannot affirm with certainty whether the Gospel is similar to this or dissimilar to that. This inability to clearly identify either continuity or discontinuity is really the genius of the Gospel; this good news from heaven is truly totally other, and yet truly and totally for people. The uniqueness of the Gospel is the encounter of Jesus of Nazareth with the person who is called by God to respond in faith: 'You are the Christ the Son of the Living God'. (Matthew 16:13-20.) The Christ who transcends all culture is nevertheless truly and uniquely for all culture. He is never completely at home, yet he seeks to be at home with us in our communities. His presence is both unsettling and blessed. The following pages are a brief description of the way in which the presence of Christ has been bringing about new reconciliation in Africa.

Although this chapter is concerned with reconciliation as it relates to the quest for an African Biblical theology, mine is not an attempt to write a theology for Africa. It is a record of what I have experienced and heard Africans do and say in this context. Most of the preaching I heard in my boyhood, which formed my earliest Christian commitments, was from first-generation Christian African lay evangelists. Their preaching influenced me. Through their message I perceived the Gospel in a manner which is precious to me.

My adult ministry has also been submerged in the African world. Those early theological insights have grown on me. I want to try to share what I think I have heard and experienced through my submersion in the African Christian experience, particularly as expressed in the East African Revival Fellowship. That Fellowship is my spiritual mentor. What I am writing is, therefore, quite subjective. I will not attempt to document or prove the accuracy of what I am writing. I will only try to report what I have experienced.

The Incarnation

Jesus is Immanuel, God with us. The Apostle John gave witness: 'The Word became flesh and lived for a while among us. We have seen his glory, the glory of the one and only Son, who came from the Father, full of grace and truth.' (John 1:14.)

And Jesus said: 'Anyone who has seen me has seen the Father.' (John 14:9.) Later the Apostle Paul reflecting back on the Christ wrote: 'He is the image of the invisible God, the firstborn over all creation. For God was pleased to have all his fullness dwell in him'. (Colossians 1 :15, 19.) In Christ, we see God revealed.

God in Christ is startling Good News. God, who was separated from humankind, has come near again. God, who seemed according to many African myths to have mysteriously withdrawn, to have become uncomfortably silent, to have absented himself from close

82

fellowship with people, this creator God of all humankind has chosen to become totally present in human community through Jesus Christ. Although every human attempt to reach God has faltered, although no tower ever built by people has been sufficiently high to arrive at the presence of God, in Christ God himself has now taken the initiative to come near; he has chosen to become present, to make himself fully known to people.

The separation between God and humankind resulted in death and disharmony, but the definitive and climatic breakthrough of God in Christ into human community is the introduction of radical peace and life. Through Jesus justice, peace, harmony, and life are recreated, because through him God has become fully present. It is no wonder that the angels in heaven sang joyously at his birth, 'Glory to God in the highest, and on earth peace to men on whom his favour rests' (Luke 2:14.)

Peace! Christ is also the breakthrough of harmony, which in Biblical understanding is anchored in the love of God. God's love, which is poured into the community of people through Christ, is harmony and peace-creating, as people open themselves to his love. In Jesus' last prayer he interceded, 'I have made you known to them, and will continue to make you known in order that the love you have for me may be in them and that I myself may be in them'. (John 17:26.)

Christ, through whom peace and harmony have broken dramatically into our community experience, is also the incarnation of life. 'In him was life, and that life was the light of men'. (John 1:4.) The African sages have always observed that the presence of God is life and immortality. In Christ that life has become fully and creatively present.

There is a disquiet about this life breakthrough. We have noted this in chapter two. In the traditional African experience the festivals when the society drew near to God were awesome events in which cleansing and peaceful preparation needed to precede the congregational festival. The coming of the Prince of Peace is similarly deeply disquieting. He is the incarnation of light, the shining one, the incarnation of truth which reveals the hidden disharmony of our

83

existence. This disquiet in the presence of Jesus is revealed in the witness of John, 'The light shines in the darkness, but the darkness has not understood it' (John 1 :5.)

The disquiet in the presence of Jesus is centered on his profound affirmation of justice. Jesus' identification with peace and harmony is anchored solidly in justice. This is revealed in Mary's song of anticipation:

He has performed mighty deeds with his arm;
  he has scattered those who are proud in their inmost thoughts.
He has brought down rulers from their thrones
  but has lifted up the humble.
He has filled the hungry with good things
  but has sent the rich away empty. (Luke 1:51-53.)

Justice with peace and righteousness! The presence of God among people is disquieting because he is the incarnation of Life!—Life which is nourished by a just-harmonious-righteous authentic human community.

The incarnation turns the traditional hierarchy of powers upside down. In Christ, God becomes servant. Philippians 2:5-8 describes the descent of Christ from the nodal point of life into the womb of creation. From God he descends into the human community, not as chief, but as the homeless one born in a cattle stable, not as a self-enhancing lord of people, but as the servant who washes his disciples' feet. In Christ, God, the nodal point of life, the hierarchical apex of power from whom all powers receive their sanction and authority, this ultimate source of all creation becomes a servant— vulnerable, present. This profound act of revolution in the power cosmology destabilizes all human structures. In the words of the Magnificat:

'He has brought down rulers fom their thrones
  but has lifted up the humble'. (Luke 1:52.)

In many African societies the breakthrough of the Gospel was destabilizing to traditional social structures. The Kingdom of Buganda is an example. In the traditional society the Kabaka had absolute power. His position was enforced by the *balubaale* cult, and upheld by a hierarchical structure of society, with serfs at the lower end of the power continuum and divinity at the apex of power. Cosmic harmony was symbolized in the Kabaka.

Within only thirteen years of the coming of the first missionaries to Buganda, the Kingdom had experienced a revolution. The transformation was a process which gained momentum as more and more people heard the Bible read with the startling Good News, that God has become incarnate as servant in Jesus Christ. Armed with this Good News, page boys in the court of the Kabaka began to rebuke some of the chiefs for having slaves. When the chiefs began to perceive the nature of the message, some of them began to dig in the fields side by side with their slaves and serfs. As the page boys and chiefs began to grasp the nature of the cosmological revolution revealed in the incarnation, they began to challenge the absolutist authority of the Kabaka, but only in areas where his authority contradicted their Christian morals and commitment.[11]

The challenge to absolute authority was so threatening to the stability of the system that a general execution of Christian page boys was ordered. Thirty-one page boys were burned to death on a great pyre at Namugongo.[12] Many other Christians died in other parts of the kingdom. As they died they cried out for all to hear: 'We are dying for freedom, for the freedom of Buganda from the tyranny of the powers which have enslaved Buganda.'[13] The death of these martyrs for freedom in Christ triggered a sequence of fast-moving events which led to the overthrow of the Kabakaship in the revolution of 1890. From that time on, the absolute power of the Kabakaship was broken forever. Although the institution was reinstated, it became thereafter a disciplined institution which received its support from the people as represented through the chiefs. The absolutism of hierarchical power was broken forever. [14]

In Christ the hierarchy of power undergoes a transformation. The chief becomes servant. It is in servanthood that his role as chief is affirmed. This incarnational revolution is profound and pervasive wherever the Gospel is genuinely experienced. Most often it is expressed in simple ways which are nevertheless deeply significant.

A friend once told me, 'Today as my wife and I were walking home from the market, I suddenly noticed that people were smiling and even laughing at us. I didn't know why, until it dawned on me that I was carrying the market basket because my wife was tired that day. Although that is against our customs, I really didn't mind the amused smiles, because I think it is right for a Christian husband to help his wife in that way when necessary.' He was the first Christian husband in that community. Today many husbands help their wives carry the basket home, but he was the first. As he told the story, I sensed that it was a spontaneous thing which he did as a subconscious response to the servant role of Jesus whom he recognized as God with us.

The hierarchical revolution does not necessarily eradicate hierarchical stability. In Buganda the Kabaka was reinstated, but with a difference. He was installed by his people, and could maintain his position thereafter only by being a sensitive servant to his people. The incarnation of the nodal Life-Giving source into history, into human community, is not the negation of Lordship, but rather the dramatic revelation that God gives himself in love to humankind. The hierarchical pyramid is turned upside down. In serving, Jesus is recognized as Lord. (Philippians 2:5-11.) It is in self-giving love that God reveals himself as the One with ultimate authority over our lives. God reigns not by might, but by right. We recognize his right to be our absolute and only authority because in Christ he has identified himself fully with our human condition as the One who lives and serves, the One who is full of 'grace and truth' (John 1:14.)

Although in Christ the nature of the hierarchy is transformed within the Christian African experience there is generally a continuing respect and affirmation of the power hierarchy. For example, church communities with a hierarchical structure are in many African communities more understandable than Christian groups with a more egalitarian structure. Thus a number of Protestant denominations which traditionally have never had a very high view of the ministry have, within the African experience, frequently developed an apostolate structure, which is different from the structures introduced by the missionaries. The hierarchy in such cases becomes a requirement for enhancing and preserving harmony and peace.

Yet, as mentioned above, the Gospel does, when Biblically perceived, transform the nature of that hierarchy. I have frequently shared in meetings of the church council in my denomination in East Africa where my bishop asked forgiveness for a wrong which he had done to us. In the traditional structure, evil is done to the elder; the elder does not commit wrongs against those lower in the hierarchy. Yet in Christ, my bishop asks us to forgive him! The bishop of Soroti, Teso, in Uganda cultivated the fields with his parishioners and fellow villagers. He has been a deeply appreciated bishop, and his diocese has thrived. Not all bishops can or should till fields, but, nevertheless, authentic Christian Church structures do reflect a deep transformation of spirit with regard to the power structure. God in Christ has become servant and vulnerable to his people. Churchly power structures also need to reflect servanthood and redemptive vulnerability. Authentic power and authority is derived from a true spirit of being a servant in the ministry.

During the severe disruption caused by the war in Zimbabwe, normal church life sometimes floundered. In some areas the eucharist was seldom shared because of the security problem for clergymen. Yet some of the Methodist clergy made a point of meeting regularly for quiet retreat and prayer. The climax of these retreats for fellowship and encouragement was, sometimes at least, feet washing. Each minister demonstrated servanthood by washing his brothers' feet; this was a sign of Christian servanthood in the midst of a war which fed on tribal and racial egoism. It was a radical in-house witness against the destructiveness of self aggrandizement.

The Crucifixion

African Christianity has also responded deeply to the crucifixion of Jesus Christ. Christ crucified is central to African preaching and faith. When discussing the crucifixion of Jesus Christ, we are treading on sacred ground; we are beginning to enter the holy of holies of Christian African experience. We enter that realm of the sacred with reverence, and we confess that we cannot adequately express in words the deep meaning of the cross for salvation and the new community.

God reveals himself as the vulnerable One in the crucifixion of Jesus Christ. In the cross the mystery deepens concerning the nature of the power of God which the incarnation reveals. Not only has the nodal Life-Giver become present among people, but he has also become vulnerable to people. In traditional belief God was generally perceived as the One who, although beneficent, was unaffected by the evil which people do. Now all of that is different. God in Christ becomes vulnerable. He is wounded by our transgression, crushed by our evil. (Isaiah 53: 5.) The evil which I do against my neighbour wounds God. In Christ, God himself experiences and absorbs the heinous evil of broken relationships, the evil which destroys life, the bitterness which becomes witchcraft and death.

God in Christ does not acquiesce to evil. In fact Jesus was crucified because he absolutely refused to avoid confrontation with the structures of evil. He encountered the powers of death and alienation. He cast out demons, even if three thousand swine died in the process. He challenged the basic assumptions of Roman imperialism by riding into Jerusalem on a donkey in the triumphal entry and by accepting the kingly praises of the people. He shattered the equanimity of the religious institutions which strangled the poor with the tenacious grip of sanctimonious avarice; he overturned the tables of the money changers in the temple. Jesus was disturbingly confrontational. He pronounced woes on the religious establishment for practising pieties which had no relevance to justice. And that is why the roof came down on his head. Christ as God with us commanded righteousness and justice. His confrontational presence was deeply disturbing; it is for this reason that he was crucified.

Yet in the death of Jesus Christ evil is defeated. It should be recalled that, in the traditional African experience, bitterness and an unforgiving attitude are the tragic cancer of the spirit which destroy life and harmony. The malicious person brings death into the community, but the person who forgives is a truly great one, and it is he who becomes a life-giving blessing to the community. Jesus is the One who is truly great for he is the One who genuinely forgives.

Jesus Christ is the Great Person and the Life-Giving One for he died without resentment. He died as a Great Person, because he had no bitterness. He suffered incredible injustice, yet with complete equanimity. The trial dialogues, his response to the persecutors, his sayings on the cross, including especially his recognition of kinship responsibilities in his arrangement for the care of his mother, all witness to an incredible presence of mind and the dignity of a truly Great Person.

The most ringing affirmation of Jesus' genuine personhood even in death is his cry, 'Father, forgive them, for they do not know what they are doing'. (Luke 23:34.) Jesus suffered without any bitterness. He forgave freely without blaming those who had tortured him. His death is a monument of greatness. Even in death he affirmed life, because he suffered without bitterness. Whenever a people invite the Spirit of Jesus the Great One to be present among them, he gives to them also the gift of forgiveness, the gift of healing, the experience of harmony and life.

The manner in which Jesus confronted injustice and accepted the consequences of suffering is normative for a Christian. It is the way any great person should live and die. Repeatedly I have heard revivalist Christians in East Africa affirm the cross as a way of life:

'I used to want the front seat of the car, but because of the cross I don't need that anymore.'

'I used to fight my husband's authoritarianism, but because of Jesus, I can now discuss matters with him, and I do not resent him these days.'

'The cross is like a long tunnel which gets smaller and smaller the further you go into it. When you begin the Christian way, you need to bend your head a little in order to enter the tunnel. But the closer you get to the cross, the lower you must bow. When you actually arrive at the cross, you discover that the tunnel is so low that you must lie with your face on the ground. All our pride is condemned at the cross.'

'The way of the cross is the way of brokenness.'

'I was terrified during the war, for fear that I would be killed. Then I saw a vision of the cross. I saw that Jesus knew how to die. Because of Jesus I experienced peace and the fear of dying left me.'

These testimonials affirm 'brokenness'. Very often the Christian calling in Africa also leads disciples of Christ into a greater awareness of the cross as a confrontation with injustice and the attendant suffering inflicted by those who are threatened by his message of love and justice. This was a prevailing theme in the Pan African Christian Leadership Assembly held in Nairobi in December 1976, which included evangelical leaders from across the African continent. Although evangelism was the announced theme of the Assembly, a central concern became the injustice of apartheid in South Africa. As that assembly struggled with the issues of injustice in Africa, the participants felt pressed by the Spirit of God into a commitment to live in self-giving confrontation with the powers and structures of evil. Christians are called to *live* within the Kingdom of God in the present, to *be* the new community, to participate fully in the experience of the incarnational breakthrough of justice, peace and life in Christ. Living that way also demands a commitment to redemptive suffering, because injustice and death oppose life, peace and harmony.

The way of the cross is deeply practical for many Christians in Africa; they experience release and victory over death. They identify deeply with Jesus who affirmed Life even in death, because of the way in which he encountered death. He died as victor. The way of the cross in human relations is the way of victory; paradoxically it is the way of life.

The Sacrifice

The New Testament refers to Jesus as the 'Lamb of God'. This is a profound revelation. In chapters two and three we have seen that the sacrificial animal in African traditional experience was chosen according to well-known and strict criteria. Often it had to be of one colour and at its prime in age. The Gikuyu description of the sacrificial event is pertinent and not uncommon. In addition to its perfection, the animal also needed to come from a good family and those who offered the sacrifice had to be people who were perfect symbols of peace.

Jesus, as the truly Great One, is the fulfilment of perfection. He is crucified, gives his life in sacrifice, the perfect Lamb provided by God himself.

We have mentioned that in Gikuyu society the day of sacrifice was called the Day of Peace. Similar concepts recur across Africa. In the sacrificial death of Christ the quest for peace in the traditional sacrificial system is fulfilled. In Christ's death, peace is established between God and the person. When Christ gave his life on the cross, the curtain in the Jewish temple in Jerusalem which obscured from view the Holy of Holies where the glory of God was traditionally present, that curtain which separated the person from the right fellowship with God, was torn in two from the top to the bottom. This brings to mind the Gikuyu seers peering through the fatty tissue of the sacrificial sheep to perceive the dim mystery of God. The torn veil then is a heavenly and universal sign that the sacrificial death of Christ has fulfilled humankind's quest for atonement through sacrifice. In Christ atonement is completed. Through his death we are accepted. In his suffering and crucifixion peace is offered forever between God and humankind. The veil is removed.

The sacrificial blood of Christ invites humankind to participate in a covenant of peace. We have described the manner in which blood was shed in sacrifice for covenant in many African societies. In many traditional societies the sacrificial blood spilled on the ground united the living-dead in ontocratic union. The living-dead, who had been buried in the ground, were united in peace through the sacrificial blood. In a similar manner the living were often united through the blood, either by sprinkling the blood on the participants or by drinking some of the blood. Blood spilled in sacrifice was a central aspect of most African covenants. A covenant sealed with sacrificial blood could never be broken; it transcended even the strongest kinship ties. If the blood of animals in traditional covenants sealed an unbreakable bond between the covenanting parties, how much more secure is the covenant bond sealed by the blood of Christ, the Lamb sent from God himself.

The blood of Christ, the perfect Lamb of God, supersedes all other covenants, for his is a more excellent sacrifice.

Sacrifice and offering you did not desire,
    but a body you prepared for me;
with burnt offerings and sin offerings
    you were not pleased.
Then I said, 'Here I am—it is written
    about me in the scroll —
I have come to do your will, O God.' (Hebrews 10:5-7.)

This Perfect One gives himself as the perfect sacrifice for sin:

The blood of goats and bulls and the ashes of a heifer sprinkled on those who are ceremonially unclean sanctify them so that they are outwardly clean. How much more, then, will the blood of Christ, who through the eternal Spirit offered himself unblemished to God, cleanse our consciences from acts that lead to death, so that we may serve the living God. (Hebrews 9:13, 14.)

The New Testament interprets the blood of Christ as establishing a New Covenant, which unites us in covenant fellowship with God and with people. The book of Hebrews is graphic in its symbolism. Christ takes his blood into the presence of God, thereby sealing the covenant between God and people. The blood also cleanses from death and establishes life. This life is experienced in covenant fellowship with God and the person. (Hebrews 9:11-14.)

The shed blood of Christ has cosmological significance. His blood is spilled in Palestine, where the continents and the races of humankind meet. All the 'living-dead' of all peoples have, therefore, been invited into communion through the shed blood of Christ. The Bible proclaims that he descended into 'the lower earthly regions'; surely the good news of the covenant extends to the ancestral 'living-dead' of all peoples. (Ephesians 4:8, 10.) Through his sacrificial death, the 'living-dead' have also been invited into covenant fellowship. (Romans 14:9.) If the 'living-dead' are reconciled, then surely the living must also live in peace !

It is among the living that the covenant takes on special practical significance. Before his crucifixion, he offered his disciples the cup saying, 'This cup is the new covenant in my blood; do this, whenever you drink it, in remembrance of me.' (I Corinthians 11:23.) Jesus shared the cup with his disciples in the context of divisiveness; they were disconcerted, knowing that a betrayer was among them. There were serious tensions within the group also, as they vied against one another for power. The egoisms of the disciples had ruptured the harmony, and death was making its entry. It was in this atmosphere of death and betrayal that Jesus introduced the cup. A new covenant! Forgiveness of sins! The cleansing of bitterness! Fellowship! Life! A covenant of his own blood!

The blood of Christ, the lamb of God, provides a cosmological covenant between God and people, God and the living-dead, the living-dead and the living, God and the living, and humankind and nature. This new covenant of peace is God's initiative. It supersedes all other covenants. It transcends all national and ethnic ties. It is a new covenant of righteousness that offers peace and harmony in the community of humankind. It is a covenant of forgiveness and life. The covenant sealed by the blood of Christ supersedes all other loyalties. (Colossians 1 :19-23.)

Communion

In Christian experience the new covenant is celebrated through eating the eucharistic bread and drinking the juice of the vine from the cup. We read, 'The Lord Jesus, on the night he was betrayed, took bread, and when he had given thanks, he broke it and said, "This is my body, which is for you; do this in remembrance of me." In the same way also he took the cup, after supper, saying, "This is the new covenant in my blood. Do this, as often as you drink it, in remembrance of me".' (I Corinthians 11:24, 25.) In traditional society the blood of the sacrificial animal was often sprinkled on the covenanters, and then the animal was usually eaten as a celebration of communion and peace.

In Christian experience the Lamb of God is the nourishment of communion and fellowship. His covenant people eat in thanksgiving; they participate in his life-giving sacrifice. He is the bread from heaven, the Lamb of God, the eternal life-giving bread in whom the banquet of life is created and nurtured. The covenant must not be taken lightly. It is a costly gift. Those who violate the covenant are judged. We read,

> Anyone who rejected the law of Moses died without mercy on the testimony of two or three witnesses. How much more severely do you think a man deserves to be punished who has trampled the Son of God under foot, who has treated as an unholy thing the blood of the covenant that sanctified him, and who has insulted the Spirit of Grace . . . It is a dreadful thing to fall into the hands of the Living God. (Hebrews 10: 28,29,31.)

The violation of the covenant is most clearly evident in sins against one's covenant brother. If one is approaching the communion table and remembers that his brother has something against him, he must go and be reconciled to his brother first, and only then should he participate in the covenant celebration. (Matthew 5:23, 24.) The participant must examine himself before communing; he incurs judgement on himself. (I Corinthians 11: 27-32.)

Many African Christians have a deep appreciation for the covenant dimensions of the sacrificial death of Christ and the eucharist as a sign and celebration of that covenant. I am impressed, for example, by the manner in which the Nairobi Mennonite congregation of which I have been a member conducts its communion services. Usually on the Saturday evening before the communion there is a preparatory service. The congregation comes together for the specific purpose of confessing sins and seeking forgiveness. The preparatory service is climaxed by washing one another's feet as a sign of servanthood and forgiveness. The meeting is concluded by joyous singing and Christian embraces of one another.

The communion is held during the Sunday worship the next morning. The messages usually deal with the new peoplehood in Christ with special emphasis on the breakdown of social barriers in Christ, a meaningful theme in an inter-ethnic urban congregation. Just before sharing the emblems, there is often a final opportunity to confess any sin which may be hindering a person from partaking. People examine themselves and some decide not to partake because of some feeling of unresolved guilt. A wrong attitude brings judgement, not blessing, in the communion experience. The bread is broken from one loaf and the wine is shared from one cup as a sign of unity in Christ. After sharing the emblems, there are hymns of praise as the congregation joyously moves about to allow each person to greet as many fellow congregational members as possible in the spirit of Christian love and fellowship. This marks the end of the service, which is followed by a thanksgiving offering. Some members have suggested that the celebration of fellowship in Christ should be climaxed by a meal. That may happen as part of a developing African awareness of the meaning of the eucharist within their heritage.

In a situation where harmony has broken down within a congregation, communion is often deferred, perhaps indefinitely. During my youth in Tanzania I recall an incident where an entire church district had come together for communion, but the African leadership advised the missionary pastor that there was disharmony, and suggested that the communion be postponed. Instead of communion the congregation was advised to confess their evil attitudes. Only recently I heard of an entire denomination which suspended communion for a period of time because of strife among the top leaders. After the issues were resolved peacefully, they celebrated a mighty communion which was a great occasion for joy and celebration.

A friend has described his experience of worshipping with the independent church of the Apostle of John Mananke in Zimbabwe. The communion can only be celebrated by those who are adjudged worthy by the Holy Spirit. The congregation comes together to assess the witness of the Spirit the day before communion. As each person attempts to enter the place of meeting, several prophets stand on either side of the entrance. If the Spirit gives sanction to the person entering, he is welcomed. If not, the prophets indicate that there is sin which must be confessed before he can enter the sanctuary. If a person is forbidden entrance, he goes into the church yard, and confesses his sins by shouting them out in the presence of God and the congregation of worshippers. After confessing, he can return and attempt to enter; if he has truthfully confessed his sins, he is welcomed; if not, he is required to return to the yard and continue the confession process. When the devotees have passed the scrutiny of the Spirit, they wash one another's hands symbolizing the cleansing which they have experienced as they helped one another discover the evil within and heard the confession. Only after ritual washing of the hands is the congregation ready for communion. The next day they reassemble for the eucharist with joy and anticipation.

The pastoral Maasai are among the most conservative peoples of East Africa. They have been largely unimpressed by modernity. Yet in some areas of East Africa, the Maasai have embraced the Gospel and incorporated the Good News into their traditional world view and culture. Father Vincent J. Donovan has described Catholic involvement in the process of indigenization in his book, *Christianity Rediscovered, An Epistle from the Maasai*.[15] As the various Maasai communities around the Loliondo Mission in Tanzania made their decision to become Christian, they chose the word *orporor* to describe the new community which they entered through baptism. *Orporor* is the age grade brotherhood. They recognize that in Christ the precious and indissoluble tie of age grade brotherhood is now extended to include all age grades, even male and female, into one new *orporor*. Old and young, male and female, all are brothers and sisters in Christ, a truly revolutionary concept!

For these Maasai the eucharist became the central event in celebrating this new experience and commitment to a brotherhood which united clan divisions into one fellowship in Christ. Father Donovan describes the eucharist as a celebration of unity in Christ. When he arrives in the nomadic village for the eucharist, he pulls a tuft of green grass from the earth, and hands it to the first Maasai elder to meet him. The grass is a sign of peace, for it is the sustenance of the community; it is the grass which nourishes the cattle which in turn provide the food for the Maasai community. Just as grass sustains the life of the community, so peace also sustains the person in community. If violence threatens in the Maasai community, a contestant may seize a tuft of grass and offer it to his opponent as a sign of peace. When the peace tuft is accepted, the opponents must make peace. And so Father Donovan takes the tuft of grass and offers it to the first elder he meets saying, 'the peace of Christ'. This tuft of grass, the sign of peace, is passed from elder to elder and from person to person throughout the village. Accepting the tuft and passing it on is a sign that one is abiding in the peace of Christ and prepared for the eucharist. If anyone or any group rejects the peace sign, the community will try to deal with the person or group redemptively immediately. But if peace eludes the community, the eucharist is deferred until another day; peace must be present before the eucharist can be celebrated, before the community can participate in communion with one another in the redemptive presence of the Lord.[16]

This congregation calls the eucharist the *orporor sinyati,* the holy brotherhood. For them it is a celebration and affirmation of union with one another in Christ. It is the celebration of new peoplehood. It is a deep affirmation of the New Testament joy of fellowship with one another in the breaking of the bread together.[17] 'The bread which we break, is it not a "communion" in the body of Christ?' (I Corinthians 10:16.)

The communion, the celebration of the 'holy brotherhood', is not without pain. Father Donovan describes the first time he celebrated the eucharist in one of the Maasai communities in Tanzania, among a people who had never thought it possible for men and women to eat together. It was an awesome moment as he handed the cup (gourd) to the woman sitting closest to him and she drank the gourd of 'holy brotherhood' in the presence of men, and then she in turn passed the gourd on to the man next to her and he also drank—the awesome and sacred celebration of the creation of new peoplehood in Christ, a people in which the peace of God has invaded the community so profoundly that now the men and women can eat together! How wonderful is the grace of God![18]

The Maasai are perceptive theologians. They began to perceive that in Christ traditional barriers are also transcended. For a people who have considerable pride, the universality of peoplehood in Christ is an awesome and almost fearful reality. In fact, perhaps few of us have ever really believed the Gospel in that way either! Father Donovan admits that one of the most painful queries these Maasai theologians have put to him was whether his own people, who have known that Gospel for centuries, really do believe that God loves everyone equally.[19] If God does love everyone equally, then the Maasai would need to stop cattle raiding, and in fact warfare must cease for all who have received the Gospel. Yet when the Maasai finally requested baptism, they did it with the full realization that they were being baptized into a universal *orporor*. Nearby enemy societies had become 'neighbour'.[20]

For the Maasai the communion is a celebration of a 'holy brotherhood' in which they are mystically united in Christ within the universal fellowship of believers. This notion that in the sacrificial death of Christ believers are united into a universal community of peace is persistently present among many Christian communities in Africa. In fact, for some African Christians, the cosmological dimension of the sacrifice of Christ is all inclusive and therefore makes it impossible for them to participate in any forms of violence or warfare. We shall describe case studies of this universalization of the peace covenant later. At this point we will note only two examples.

Several years ago I was involved in Church mission in an eastern African community which had never heard the Gospel before. A policeman was among the early Christian believers in that community. Several weeks after making his commitment to Christ, there was a riot in the town, and he and his battalion were ordered to shoot at the rioters. He began to obey the order but then felt constrained to resist it. The commander was furious. Although almost totally illiterate theologically, the young man later interpreted his hesitancy in Biblical terms. He said that because of Jesus Christ he could not shoot at those people.

A Kenyan churchman told me much the same thing concerning his spiritual pilgrimage during the Mau Mau freedom war. He said, 'I could not take a gun to defend myself because I was already protected by the blood of Christ. I told the officer who wanted me to take a gun that I could never do so, because the blood of Jesus Christ was shed for both the black man and the white man, and therefore we are now all brothers. How could I shoot at a man for whom Christ had died?' He went on to say that the white officer wept tears as the African church man spoke to him of that kind of covenant of brotherhood.

The Resurrection

Professor John S. Mbiti suggests that the eschatological impact of the resurrection on the African perception of time is revolutionary. The resurrection of Christ is a sign of the eschatological consummation of the Kingdom of God at the *parousia*. It therefore explodes the myth of the 'golden age' in the *Zamani,* introducing instead the revolutionary concept of fulfilment in the future, a future, nevertheless, which has already begun.[21] In recent years there has been considerable research and reflective writing concerning the implications of the resurrection for a people's historical perceptions, whether they be African, European, or Asian.[22] Within the context of this broad based theological reflection, it would seem that Professor Mbiti is probably right. The resurrection explodes all forms of cyclical history and introduces instead the concept of hope, fulfilment and purpose.

Nevertheless, there is a strong impression that at this point in Africa's theological ferment the resurrection has far greater existential impact as an immediate spiritual reality than as an eschatological hope. I have heard many missionaries preach about the future hope and a final judgement. I have seldom heard an African preach on this subject. I have seldom, if ever, heard a missionary preach on the relationships of the resurrection to the present spiritual powers, but I have often heard Africans preach about that dimension of the resurrection reality. It is the power encounter of the resurrection which has apparently gripped the African continent far more than the hope for a future bodily resurrection. I do not mean that the historical dimension is not important. Certainly it is, but at the moment the resurrection is speaking mostly about the triumph of Christ over the spirits in the present. For the church in Africa the eschaton is indeed at hand; it has invaded the domain of the powers.

We have already commented on the manner in which disharmonious relationships were the seedbed for spirit possession, witchcraft and sorcery. These forms of dehumanization and death were linked to the death processes of envy, jealousy, anger, bitterness, or hate. These attitudinal evils are open invitations for death processes. However, the resurrection of Jesus Christ is the ultimate triumph over all forms of death. The death and resurrection of Christ is proof that the power of evil and death is broken. He did not passively avoid encounter; he overturned the tables of the money changers; he devastatingly challenged the unjust structures of Jewish and Roman societies, both in their personal and corporate expressions. Because he is the perfect and full incarnation of life, he never compromised with the powers of death. It is for that reason that the authorities were determined to crucify him.[23] The powers of injustice, disharmony and death rejected the Life-Giver.

But Jesus died triumphantly. The powers of death have been defeated through the Spirit of the cross. Jesus confronted the evil powers of injustice, disharmony and death with selfgiving, persistent love and without bitterness or revenge. He forgave even while dying. In his death he affirmed life without in the least yielding to the ultimate destroyer, bitterness. By thus dying, Jesus destroyed death. He arose from the dead, a victor over the evil forces which had vehemently tried to destroy him. The resurrection is therefore an assurance of hope. The spirit of Jesus empowers the disciple of Jesus to live in harmony and freedom as Jesus did, to both confront and love his enemy, to suffer for the sake of righteousness, justice and peace but not become bitter in his sufferings, to triumph over death. Suffering is not acquiescence to death; it is rather the necessary consequence of encounter with the powers of death. Suffering is the means through which God leads his people to triumph over death.

The resurrection is therefore a ringing affirmation that justice will prevail, that life cannot be defeated. The people of God, who patiently confront and resist evil, will be rewarded. Although they may walk in the valley of death, they will be led out of that valley in triumph.

The significance of the resurrection extends throughout the spiritual cosmos. All the deathprone spiritual forces are defeated through the triumph of Christ. He has been elevated to Lordship over all principalities and powers. (Ephesians 1:19-23.) All the spiritual beings are under his lordship. Their ultimate power is now dramatically broken. As the resurrected Lord, he encounters the powers and puts them to flight. The Gospel, in the words of Dr. Donald R. Jacobs, is a 'power encounter'.[24] The Apostle Paul writes, 'This is why it says, "When he ascended on high, he led captives in his train and gave gifts to men," . . . He who descended is the very one who ascended higher than all the heavens, in order to fill the whole universe.' (Ephesians 4:8, 10.)

This encounter and victory over the powers of death is dramatic and decisive. It is a fact of African Christian experience. I grew up in an area of East Africa where the Gospel was being preached for the first time. The power of the spirits was still believed in strongly and spiritual forces were still present in great power; serious attempts were made to curse to death one of the African evangelists whose actions had alienated some of the spirit specialists. All the village homesteads in those days had high cactus hedges surrounding them, allegedly to keep out witches at night.

Then the Gospel began to break through. A common scene in the little church became the burning of charms with the ringing witness: 'Christ is Lord over all, and therefore I do not need these things to protect me any more.' I often remember testimonies given in church by new Christians which would go something like this: 'I used to fear the powers of death but praise God, I have destroyed my charms, and my fears are gone. Truly Jesus is the victor over the powers!' These were new Christians giving witness to a theology and experience which the missionaries hardly understood, for spirits were not a very lively part of missionary cosmology. This was African 'lay' theology in the making. These 'new-born' Christians taught me more in my impressionable teenage years about the reality of spiritual encounter than I have ever learned in all my subsequent studies of psychology and spirituality in western universities.

A dramatic sign that the spirits had been put to flight was the tearing down of the cactus hedges. Slowly at first, but then all across the countryside, the impregnable cactus hedges around the village homesteads were burned down or destroyed. They were needed no more. Christ had taken the spirits away in a great triumphal train. The resurrected Christ is the triumph of life over all forms of death. The spirits who feed on the malicious have been subdued forever.

What happens to the living-dead in the light of the resurrection? For many African Christians they do not entirely cease to matter, although they no longer hold a central position in the life of the community. A new born baby may be in the habit of crying excessively. In a vision one of the departed may request to have the baby named after him or her. Giving the baby the ancestral name suggested in the vision seems to cure the baby's discomfort. In parish work stories like this are repeated again and again. The significant difference, however, is that this sort of benevolent interchange is not tinged with the fear which previously characterized malicious spirit manifestations; similarly, the power of the fearsome sorcerers is broken. It is clear that something shattering has happened to the powers through the death and resurrection of Christ. All powers are under his Lordship.

A lively theological issue, which anyone encounters while teaching theology in an African community, is, 'what is the relationship between Christ and the living-dead?'

The response I most frequently hear from African Christians is that the living-dead are invited to share in the experience of redemption, that it is the intention of God that they are redeemed. Is this what the Apostle Paul had in mind when he quoted the Psalmist, saying, 'When he (Christ) ascended on high, he led captives in his train and gave gifts to men?' (Ephesians 4:8 NIV.)

Does this suggest that the risen Christ has redeemed and captivated hosts of the living-dead and taken them with him into glory in a great triumph procession? It is difficult to state this reality theologically, but, nevertheless, the witness of the Spirit of Christ in the African experience seems to be that hosts of the living-dead have become part of the cloud of witnesses (Hebrews 12:1) who glorify and exalt Christ; therefore, the living and the living-dead, are invited to share together the life of the redeemed community. If the righteous living-dead have been united in communion with Christ, then the living are certainly also invited to commune together in the presence of Jesus, the resurrected One. If hosts of the living-dead of peoples everywhere are being united together in Christ, then the diverse communities of the living should also be in peace.

There is a further mystery concerning the nature of Christ's triumph over the evil powers. Certainly he is triumphant because God has raised him from the dead and exalted him 'far above all rule and authority and power and dominion. ...' (Ephesians 1:21.) But probably the power of Christ in overcoming the powers of evil is especially experienced in his transforming, forgiving grace.

Without Christ's help it is exceedingly difficult to forgive. Africans have always recognized that an unforgiving spirit is the source of all sorts of malevolence, including spirit possession, witchcraft and murder. We have discussed some traditional techniques which attempted to cope with these death expressions of attitudinal evil. But the traditional cure was not adequate. In spite of the sophisticated techniques which were used to cope with this problem, the thorn hedges never went down around the family homesteads to let out the evil. Traditional covenant and sacrificial systems were not a sufficient remedy for the magnitude of the problem. My Tanzanian bishop tells me that in his pre-Gospel boyhood days, 'Witchcraft was a terrible scourge. It was destroying our people.'

The good bishop goes on to say, however, that in Christ a mighty deliverance has swept the land, for in Christ forgiveness and healing are possible. Through his supreme act of forgiveness we also can forgive. Through Christ attitudinal malevolence is neglected, and thus the source of witchcraft and spirit possession is dried up.

Witchcraft withers and dies among a people who are forgiven and who forgive.

A number of years ago a murderer was present in a church service in which my parents were participating. No one knew he was a murderer, but at the close of the service, he arose and publicly confessed his sins. Then he turned to the woman whose husband he had murdered and asked her to forgive him. With tears of compassion and forgiveness she arose and reached out her hands to the murderer of her husband and forgave him. The entire congregation burst into songs of praise. Witchcraft can never take root in a community of faith which forgives and loves like that! The forgiving grace of God in Christ destroys death by bringing healing to the very source of death, the inner spirit of man. In the words of St. Paul, 'I have been crucified with Christ; it is no longer I who live, but Christ who lives in me; and the life I now live in the flesh I live by faith in the Son of God, who loved me and gave himself for me.' (Galatians 2:20.)

The life-giving fellowship covenant which Christ created through his sacrificial death is confirmed and sealed forever through his eternal resurrection. The covenant in his blood is the eternal covenant of life. The resurrection is the proof that the person in joyous covenant fellowship with God and his fellowpersons is in the process of experiencing life eternal. The covenant affirms the eternal personhood of humanity.

The Presence

Africans have always been aware of that other presence which encompasses the experience of the person in community. In tradititional faith that presence was the ancestral spirits, and the presence was so pervasive that even in eating, water was poured in libation and morsels of food shared in appreciation and thanksgiving.

In Christian experience the ancestral presence loses some of its central importance. While its presence may still be recognized to some extent, as for example in the naming of children, nevertheless,

I have seen repeatedly that when a home accepts the Gospel, the ancestral awareness is often replaced or sublimated by an awareness of the Presence of the Holy Spirit, the Spirit of Jesus. He becomes the loving and affirming Presence in all Christian fellowship.

An awareness of the presence of the Holy Spirit permeates African Christian experience. Even a cup of tea served in the restuarant is an occasion for prayer, an acknowledgement that in the fellowship of drinking that tea the presence of the Spirit is needed for blessing and enrichment. At the beginning of a journey and at its end, prayers are offered in supplication and thanksgiving for the Presence. And in the fellowship of believers I have often observed statements such as, 'The Lord is here', or 'Praise the Lord', or 'Let's pray'. There is often a sensitive concern for words or attitudes which may offend the Presence.

Decision-making processes are often conducted with help from this Presence. A potentially divisive issue must be approached with sensitivity. Sometimes a group will speak parabolically, laying the groundwork for a more direct approach to the problem. This is because there is an agonizing awareness that, if the group is not exceedingly careful, the wrong approach to the issue could offend the Presence and the harmony of the fellowship would be disrupted. Only after there is an awareness that the community is committed to the Presence of the Spirit of Jesus are they ready to engage in the issue directly. Prayers of commitment must precede the encounter. If it becomes clear during a heated discussion that the Spirit of Jesus is being grieved, the isssue will be left for the present until the Spirit is ready for further discussion. Such a postponement of decision is often affirmed by the expression 'We will now commit the matter to prayer and to the Lord'. The maintenance of harmony in fellowship with the Presence of the Spirit of Jesus is far more urgent than any resolution of the issue could ever be.

The deep appreciation for the Presence of the Spirit is an existential affirmation of trinitarian theology, not, however, necessarily in the classical Chalcedonian formulations. African trinitarian theology is a relational reality. It is more in harmony with Augustine's perception of the Trinity as the divine fellowship of love than

Origen's more philosophical definitions. The Trinity is an expression of the harmony of God within himself. It is divine community. In Christ that loving divine harmony becomes incarnate into the community of humanity, for God intends to recreate within human community the divine symphony of unity, love, and harmony.

In Christ the triune expression of the love of God, of divine unity, communion, harmony, life-giving and life-sustaining community, is incarnated into the human experience. Through the Holy Spirit that love becomes personally and communally present among us. The Trinity, therefore, concerns practical human community today. The Trinity is a revelation of the manner in which I should relate to my neighbour. It is God's revelation of his gracious intentions for practical community relationships. The presence of the Spirit in Christian fellowship is the Presence of the harmonious self-giving love of God within us and among us, love as revealed in the Father as Creator, the Son as Saviour, and the Spirit as Presence. This is *agape* love, a precious gift of authentic life-giving community from God himself.

The Church
In African traditional experience, each particular society was a community of faith. Although there was in most communities a recognition of the universality of God and the commonalty of all people, each particular society participated in its own ontocracy of faith and practice. We have noted in chapter three that, although strangers could be incorporated through covenant, the expression of faith in a community was never perceived in universal terms. It was either a Gikuyu, or a Luo, or an Akan expression of faith.

However, Christ breaks in from outside the traditional community structures. He is genuinely 'other'. His 'otherness' is an affirmation of his universality. In Christ people are invited into a new, other, universal fellowship of faith, a huge univeral community which encompasses peoples from all around the world. For many Africans the universal dimension of the Church has been very attractive.

Through baptism the believer becomes a member of a new and precious universal community.

Not long ago I heard an African preaching a baptismal sermon. He briefly recounted the story of his life. He had been born in a remote little village in Ethiopia. As a herdsboy, he became intrigued by the little church which was taking root in his community. During the Sunday worship he would bring the goats near the worshippers and listen to the preaching. Then he believed and was finally baptized. He told of how that event introduced him to a marvellous world-wide community. Because of baptism he is now welcome in any part of the world. Wherever he travels, all he needs to do is look in the telephone directory, find the name of a local church, call the pastor, and say, 'I am a Christian from Ethiopia'. He immediately forms a relationship, and always he has been hosted and loved loyally. This new and universal community of faith, in whose fellowship no believer is a stranger, in the Church. By its nature it is more accommodating to people seeking for more universal relationships than any local expressions of faith could ever allow.

The transcultural nature of the Church has placed the African Church in a unique and significant position in the modern process of nation formation in Africa south of the Sahara. In many new nations the Church is the primary transcultural community. It is the inner force which holds the nation together. In the post-independence period, the Church continues to bear a major responsibility in helping to oil the inter-ethnic experience required of modern nationhood.

Several examples may be instructive. In Ghana the Church played a significant role in the confrontation and reconciliation process which finally led to the dissolution of military rule and the transition to civilian government in 1979. In Kenya there have been several major political crises which the nation has faced since independence. Several times, when it seemed that multi-ethnic rivalries might destroy national unity, the Church stepped in to affirm the unity of the Kenyan people. The witness of the Church in the interest of national harmony and reconciliation has been a stabilizing factor throughout the Kenyan (post-independence) nation. In both pre-and post-Amin Uganda, the Church has also played a crucial role in the process of national reconciliation and stability. (See pages 136-139 for an account of Christian witness in Uganda.) In fact the government urged the Church to organize revival meetings throughout the nation as a mighty testimony to reconciliation and moral commitment. In Sudan, the All Africa Conference of Churches was deeply involved in the 1972 Addis Ababa peace accord, which helped to bring an end to the Civil War which had devastated the southern region for more than a decade. The Church has also become a principal agent in reconstruction projects, as in the case of Sudan. Similarly, Church officials in Kenya and Tanzania have met on many occasions, both among themselves and with the respective government leaders, in an effort to solve the long-standing closure of the border (in 1977) between Kenya and Tanzania. These quiet and unpublicized meetings were an attempt to give witness to the intention of God for all people to live in a community without barriers, a community in which all divisive elements have been removed. The Church was fundamentally involved in the astonishing transformation of South Africa away from apartheid and white minority rule.

The Church in post-independence Africa has been more involved in being truly rooted in the local community than in ecumenism and, at the grassroots level, it can be admitted that even in urban centres, the Church is still organized along ethnic lines. In the city it is mostly the Church which preserves the traditional ethnic values and provides an 'ethnic' home for the 'lost' individual. News from 'home' is shared in the congregation. Burials, weddings and other social commitments, which require group help, are organized from this base. In this way the Church has played an important role in cushioning the cultural shocks brought about by a forcible introduction of a foreign culture and strange, complex economic and commercial ways of conducting national life.

However, as we saw above, the Church through its leadership has also responded to the needs of national unity when these seemed threatened. The attitudes of the Churches' officials have influenced the congregations in their charge, and although these congregations are still distinctly ethnic in their composition, their outlook has been towards national unity. Thus the Church has a dual and important role to play in post-independent Africa.

The Church: A Sign of the Kingdom of God

The Church is called by God to be a witness among the nations; it is called to be a redemptive and reconciling witness, a people who reveal that the Kingdom of God has begun, that the new community in Christ is at hand, that God has already begun, to bring all things together in Christ, that the life-giving recreation of authentic, harmonious relationships is already a reality. The Church is called to be an indication, an authentic revelation of God's gracious intention 'to unite all things in him (Christ) things in heaven and things on earth' (Ephesians 1:9.)

Tragically the Church in Africa has sometimes been a very imperfect sign. The failures of missionary or colonialist Christians are well known and documented. Elaboration here is not necessary; only several examples are noted. In Kenya the missionary movement and colonialist policies sometimes converged into a far too cozy relationship. In Mozambique, the dominant Church structures largely resisted the independence movement of the 1960's. In South Africa the Dutch Reformed Church was a bulwark of racism for many decades. In Kenya churchly dissension has on occasion even led to strife and violence, as, for example, the *Johera* (people of love) versus the *Joremo* (people of Blood) schism of the 1950's. In Chad Christian communities in the southern part of the country have engaged in the killing of Muslims. In the 1994 Rwanda genocide the institutional church was tragically compromised. In Liberia too many church leaders have been in complicity with the brutal civil war that commenced in 1989.

In many African societies the Church has contributed to a serious fracturing of traditional community structures, to such an extent among some peoples that the traditional mechanisms for communicating values have almost totally collapsed. In some situations the Church has been unkindly and devastatingly critical of traditional culture and has been guilty of robbing peoples of their sense of dignity and worth. The litany of failure is painful. The Church has too often been a sign of broken community and death. Rather than bringing healing, the Church has often contributed to the disease of brokenness and disharmony. Rather than being a community redeemed from sin, it has been a community of sinfulness, brokenness, alienation.

However, as we have already mentioned, there is another side to the picture. There are countless disciples of Jesus in the African continent who have always been a light, a witness to reconciliation, a sign that the grace of God is present. These communities of justice, peace, and reconciliation are authentic and attractive signs of the presence of the Kingdom of God. These communities of faith give witness to Jesus Christ, who is the authentic presence of the new community, the Kingdom of God in reality.

Because of Jesus Christ, a multitude of Christians in Africa live in joyous faith and hope. Even in situations where economic pressures or political structures may seem formidably arrayed against authentic personal growth and community, they live in joy and hope. They are stubbornly certain that through Jesus the victory of authentic community is absolutely assured. The process has already begun within history. Its consummation is certain.

I am often amazed at both the tenacity and the patience with which African Christians work towards the promise of *parousia,* that seal of hope and eternal triumph of peace and justice. Every African Christian I had ever spoken to concerning the apartheid system in South Africa was absolutely sure that the system would die. They knew that the system was doomed.

This absolute confidence in the triumph of justice and peace is doubtlessly informed by the traditional African belief in God as the one who establishes peace and justice. (See Chapter I.) This traditional belief is affirmed and expanded through Jesus Christ. In Christ justice is assured. Did not Jesus say that he has come to establish justice and righteousness?

Many Christian communities in Africa believe that God intends his Church to be a witness against injustice. The Church must confront these evil powers, even though in the confrontation suffering is experienced. But suffering is redemptive among the people of God and by it the powers of death are defeated. Unjust social structures are manifestations that the human experience is trapped in death processes which must be brought under the Lordship of Christ; they must be defeated in his name. Victory is certain because of the nature of Jesus and his mission on earth.

It is through the presence and witness of the Church that God begins to recreate the world order. The Church should be a redeemed and reconciling community among the nations; in this way the Church becomes a sign that the Kingdom of God has broken through. The Church should be a destabilizing witness, a sure word within human community that all unjust and evil systems which breed death and dehumanization are under judgement.

The witness of the Church to the presence of the Kingdom should also be experienced in the whole spectrum of human and economic development. From the planting of Christianity in sub-Saharan Africa right into the dawn of the twenty-first century, the Church has often been a sign of humanization at every level of life; freedom to the slave was a nineteenth century sign of the presence of the Kingdom. After that battle was won, the Church moved on to serve other human needs particularly in education and health care. By the time the sub-Saharan peoples had gained independence as modern nations, 80 per cent of all education was church-related. Throughout the continent the Church has been the vanguard of modern secular education.

In the post-independence period the emphasis has shifted from education to community development. In many African countries the Church has become the most viable instrument, and in some situations the only catalyst, for community development. These wide-ranging ministries include desert control, home industries development, urban housing and energy conservation programmes. The churches of Kenya have even recently convened a significant international conference on alternate sources of energy!

After independence when Tanzania began its experiment with African Socialism, the government asked the Church to help encourage the spirit of socialism. The founding father of the Tanzania nation, Julius Nyerere has pointed out, that Tanzanian socialism, while genuinely African, is also deeply Christian. If the Church's role, then, is to witness to the rule of peace and justice, and if its presence should be felt in all spheres of life, then its presence should be just the kind of leaven which the Tanzania society needs in order to fulfil its aims in nation building.

These ministries of the Church are signs of the Kingdom. Salvation in the African perspective is holistic. The person is not dichotomized into spiritual and physical entities. He is a whole person. The person needs salvation. In Kenya wherever Christian community development people serve, prayers, preaching and digging are intermingled. The Gospel is good news for the whole man. African churchpersons frequently express dismay at the approach to human needs which characterizes western church agencies. If one wants to dig water wells to help the nomadic poor, he must go to one Church agency, but if the quest is for assistance in preaching to those same people, then he needs to go to the division of evangelism. This dividing of the person into physical and spiritual parts makes no theological or practical sense in the African experience.

Jesus proclaimed that the Kingdom of God is at hand; it is God's gracious loving intention to unite all creation in Christ, to redeem and heal any broken community, to recreate an authentic life-sustaining community for people, to bring loving harmony into all relationships: God—man—nature. That is the Good News which Jesus preached. In Christ there is redemption for all creation. The Church is called to be a living witness of that redemptive breakthrough. The Church is the new community which stands in direct continuity with Jesus' announcement in the Nazareth synagogue nearly 2,000 years ago:

The Spirit of the Lord is on me,
    because he has anointed me
to preach good news to the poor,
    He has sent me to proclaim freedom
for the prisoners

and recovery of sight for the blind,
to release the oppressed,
to proclaim the year of the Lord's favour (Luke 4: 18, 19).

The synagogue audience was intense with expectation. Then Jesus announced with conviction and authority, 'Today this scripture is fulfilled in your hearing'. (Luke 4:21). The Church is called to speak and act with the same authority today!

The theology and experience of justice, reconciliation and peace in human experience is never a tidy affair. The process always goes on. We are always becoming, and sometimes regression is our experience. There are also other currents within life's stream.

I have tried to describe some of the currents within African theological reflection which have helped to carry me along. I have not said much about the eddies and whirlpools, the marshes and shallows, or the back waters. I have deliberately narrowed my reflection and described those aspects of theological processing and movement which seem to me to relate particularly to the recreation of the person and the community of persons.

REFERENCES

1. Walbert Buhlman, *The Coming of the Third Church,* New York, Orbis, 1977.
2. John V. Taylor, *The Primal Vision,* London, S.C.M. 1963.
3. Aylward Shorter, *African Culture and the Christian Church,* London, Geoffrey Chapman, 1973.
4. Harry Sawyerr, *God: Ancestor or Creator?* London, Longman, 1970.
5. John S. Mbiti, *New Testament Eschatology in an African Background,* London, S.P.C.K., 1978.
6. E. Bolaji Idowu, *African Traditional Religion,* London SC.M., 1973.
7. Byang Kato, *Theological Pitfalls in Africa,* Nairobi, Evangel, 1974.
8. Kwesi Dickson and Paul Ellingwood, *Biblical Revelation and African Beliefs,* Maryknoll, Orbis, 1969.
9. John S. Pobee, *Toward an African Theology,* Nashville, Abingdon, 1979.
10. Sergio Torres and Virginia Fabella, eds., *The Emergent Gospel,* New York, Orbis, 1976, 1-99.
11. W.B. Anderson, *The Church in East Africa,* 1840-1974, Dodoma, Central Tanganyika Press, 1977, 27-8.
12. Ibid., 29.
13. Ibid., 32.
14. Ibid., 34-45.
15. Vincent J. Donovan, *Christianity Rediscovered, An Epistle from the Maasai,* Notre Dame, Fides, Clarentine, 1978.
16. Ibid., 122-8.
17. Ibid., 122-3.
18. Ibid., 119-22.
19. Ibid., 41-9.
20. Ibid., 81-97.
21. John S. Mbiti, *African Religions and Philosophy,* London, Heinemann, 1971, 15-28.
22. One of the most astute studies of the significance of the Gospel for a people's perspective on time is: *Honest Religion for Secular Man,* by J.E. Lesslie Newbigin, London, S.C.M., 1966.
23. John H. Yoder, *The Politics of Jesus,* Grand Rapids, Eerdmans, 1972.
24. Donald R. Jacobs, 'Culture and the Phenomena of Conversion', *Gospel in Context,* July, 1978, 7-9.
25. Taylor, op. cit., 164-71.

O Lamb of God
Who takes away all sin,
O Lamb of God,
Have mercy on us sinners,
O Lamb of God.

O Lamb of God,
Who takes away all sin,
O Lamb of God,
Grant us your peace,
O Lamb of God.

.A Maasai Hymn

Chapter V

LIVING IN PEACE

April, 1994, was tumultuous. In unforgettable drama that month revealed the paradox of our human situation. April 26-29 1994 the world rejoiced in awesome astonishment at the miracle of the transformation from white minority rule in South Africa through free and open elections. However, also in April, 1994, the world was appalled by the genocidal massacres in Rwanda resulting in some two million refugees fleeing into neighbouring Zaire and Tanzania.

Forces of Disharmony
These forms of paradox mirror both the earnest quest for peace, reconciliation, justice and harmonious community in Africa, as well as the tremendous social, economic, political and cultural pressures which threaten to erode the fabric of the community. We cannot fully appreciate the brave efforts many are making to achieve reconciliation and cohesion, without at the same time being aware of the forces which erode the very foundations on which a viable community must be built. We cannot comment on all of the corrosive pressures, but several contributors to disharmonious relationships should be noted, providing, of course, that we recognize that all societies need to cope with disintegrative forces.

A major challenge facing the African community is the transition from small-scale society to large-scale national and international relationships.[1] The mechanisms which were quite able to maintain a small-scale community in a relatively harmonious manner are often not able to cope with large-scale inter-relationships. There are many dimensions to this problem. For example, in a traditional small-scale society, the hierarchy of power provided appropriate mechanisms for stability, authority and role definitions. However, can the hierarchies of several dozen small-scale societies be coalesced into one national community? What happens to the traditional power hierarchy of each community, and how can a viable structure of authority emerge which is sufficiently stable to bring about a sense of national consciousness? How can a newly created national hierarchy

116

command loyalty and respect, without forcefully demanding it? The normal pattern in post-independent Africa has been the creation of single party states. How does a single party state avoid the pitfalls of autocracy and the abrogation of human rights in the interests of stability and unity? These are difficult issues. Considering the depth of the issues, many African states have had a remarkably good record; stability, unity, authority and human rights are being achieved.

For many decades the apartheid system in southern Africa was a cancer in the soul of Africa. Apartheid was, in a special way, a Christian problem. Both the Africans and the whites are generally committed to Christianity. Yet the black perception of Christian faith was vastly different from that which was practised by the Dutch Reformed Church in South Africa. For African Christians (as well as a growing number of white Christians in South Africa), apartheid was a tragic perversion of the new community in Christ. Yet for many years, in spite of attempts to start a dialogue with the system, the racist policies of the government persisted. How does one encounter that kind of a system creatively and effectively? For many Africans violence seemed to be the only alternative. Violence was used against the racist regimes in Mozambique, Angola, and Zimbabwe, and these were finally overthrown. Yet violence breeds violence. In both Angola and Mozambique the cycle of violence continued for several decades after the colonial regime had collapsed. Is there no better way?

There are also other forms of community perversion. How should one deal with an evil person? In traditional society such people were, rightly or wrongly, regarded as witches and were dealt with severely, including being killed. The irredeemable evil person needed to be eradicated. The cancer of disharmony had to be exorcised in order that equilibrium and harmony be maintained. But who is the evil person in modern society? The thief? The one who bribes? The corrupt politician? The liar? The one who leads an opposition political party? The one who questions the integrity of government? What represents an authentically destructive challenge to a community? And how should society cope with these challenges? How does one balance human rights and the dignity of the person, with the very real need to maintain the life-sustaining harmony of the person in community? Sadly, some leaders in modern Africa have used the sword to take life rather than to preserve it; for them the evil person was whoever did not appear to be totally loyal to the rule of the government. For these autocratic leaders any form of dissent is treason against the welfare of the community as a whole. Whenever that happens, the community itself turns in on itself and begins to wither away.

Sometimes the 'evil one' is synonymous with one small-scale community in the new nation-state. There is a special temptation for small-scale societies vying for position in a large-scale nation-state to explain away the leadership's weaknesses and excesses, when these are pointed out, as fabrications by those who are against the government. The ensuing tensions, have at times become intolerable, in which case a genocidal explosion is possible, as has unfortunately happened in a few African countries since independence.

We do not want to dwell extensively on the potential for community distortions. These several aspects of potential disharmony have been mentioned as a backdrop for this chapter, which is concerned with the manner in which Christians across the African continent have been helping to bind the wounds, create unity, reconcile and bring peace and justice in societies where these aspects have been severely strained. The Christian commitment to harmony is often remarkable, especially when described against a background of forces of disharmony.

We could, of course, also describe sad instances of Church failure to bring about harmony. At times the Church itself has contributed to the potential for disintegration. We have already mentioned several examples of Christian failure. These are serious, a betrayal of the Christian calling. Nevertheless, in this chapter we are describing examples of the Church in a ministry of reconciliation. I believe that the commitment and the effectiveness of the Church's witness for and participation in peace and reconciliation in Africa represents a synthesis of the African traditional commitments to peace and the Gospel of peace as revealed in Jesus Christ. The following are a few examples of this witness.

The Church of Jesus Christ on Earth Through Simon Kimbangu

At N'Kamba in Lower Zaire (Congo) there is a fine wood carving of Simon Kimbangu; this carving identifies the prophet of Lower Zaire with Simon of Cyrene, who helped to carry the cross of Jesus.[2] Who is Simon Kimbangu? Who is this man who in his suffering and ministry laid the foundations of one of Africa's most dynamic Christian denominations, a church of more than 1,000,000 members, the Church of Jesus Christ on Earth through the Prophet Simon Kimbangu?

According to Kimbanguist legends, Simon Kimbangu received at least two visions of Christ before his call to prophet-hood. In each vision Christ appeared as neither black nor white. He was the colourless One, the Saviour who came to redeem all humankind. The visions have deeply penetrated Kimbanguist theology. In Christ there is no black nor white, and therefore all races are called by God to relate to one another as equal brethren.[3]

In 1918 Simon Kimbangu received his first call to prophet-hood. He resisted the call of the Lord for three years, but then, when only in his early thirties, he yielded to the voice of God. Immediately, on 6 April, 1921, his prophetic ministry began. With great joy thousands of people in the area around the prophet's home at N'Kamba turned to Christ, and many remarkable healings took place. In Simon Kimbangu the people saw a dramatic revelation of Jesus Christ's power incarnate, fully present in the African community. The miracles revealed that Jesus was not simply an ancient historical person; he had become truly present among the peoples of Lower Zaire.

Simon Kimbangu ministered publicly for only a little more than five months. The joyous spontaneity of the movement of the Spirit of God in Lower Zaire troubled some of the ecclesiastical authorities, and the Belgian colonial officials were also disturbed about the potentiality for insubordination to white colonial rule by a movement which was so joyously human and free. The local Catholic leadership, especially, urged the colonial officials to act promptly against the movement. A Belgian military detachment was sent into the N'Kamba area, but Simon Kimbangu and his followers did not resort to any forms of violence. Nevertheless, the colonial officer in charge of the soldiers who bivouacked in N'Kamba was chagrined because the prophet insisted on praying before speaking with the military commander; or was it the reading of the story of David and Goliath to the commander which most angered the Belgian officer! In any event, on 6 June, only two months after the prophet had begun his mission, the Belgian authorities ordered his arrest.

Simon Kimbangu and several of his followers escaped arrest by fleeing. He continued his ministry for another three months in Mbanza-Nsanda. This was a time of considerable deprivation. Even food was scarce, and the Belgian authorities were seeking everywhere for the prophet. Some of his followers were detained and rigorously interrogated. Nevertheless, he used these three months to teach a small group of his followers, and especially an inner cluster of twelve.

This period of seclusion came to an abrupt end when in September Simon Kimbangu received a word from the Lord that he should return to his home and face arrest. This call reminds one of Jesus, who was also called to go to Jerusalem. In fact, N'Kamba is called the New Jerusalem among Kimbanguist Christians. Both Jesus Christ and Simon Kimbangu voluntarily accepted unjust arrest in 'Jerusalem'. Foreseeing the suffering which was ahead for him and his followers, Kimbangu urged his disciples to practise the Sermon on the Mount literally. He commanded them to utterly renounce violence. Like Jesus at his arrest in Gethsemane, Simon Kimbangu turned away from any forms of violence. He urged his followers to face suffering courageously and never to repay evil with evil.

He gave himself up for arrest on 12 September, 1921. The spot where he was arrested is where the steps begin which lead upward to the mausoleum where the remains of Simon Kimbangu have been buried. Several of his followers, as well as his wife and three young sons, were also taken from N'Kamba. Later the authorities permitted his wife, Mwilu Marie, to return home, but they tried to arrange for the re-education of the eldest boy, a seven-year-old, by sending him to a Catholic school.

Events moved rapidly. On 3 October, Simon Kimbangu was sentenced to death after receiving 120 strokes. Perhaps because of strong protests by some Church authorities in Zaire, the death penalty was commuted to life imprisonment by King Albert of Belgium. But that same month the prophet was deported over two thousand kilometres from home to prison in Lubumbashi in Katanga Province. He received the 120 strokes and spent the next thirty years in prison, mostly in solitary confinement.[5]

Because of his exemplary conduct in prison, there was an attempt to have his jail sentence reduced, but there was no dispensation forthcoming from higher authorities. He died as an imprisoned martyr on 12 October, 1951. His family was not even informed of his death, but providentially his youngest son, Joseph Diangienda, saw a vision of his father who said, 'I now live with God in heaven'.[6] It was in this way that the family first received word of the death of the prophet. Acting promptly after that vision, Joseph Diangienda was able to gain possession of the remains of his father. Kimbanguist Christians see a parallel between this and Joseph in the Bible who claimed the remains of his father from Egypt and went to Canaan to bury him there. So also Joseph, son of Simon Kimbangu, reclaimed the remains of his father from the colonial authorities and transported them over two thousand kilometres back home to N'Kamba for burial. Subsequently thousands of pilgrims have come to the burial shrine in the 'New Jerusalem' yearly to be inspired by the life of this suffering servant of Jesus, Simon Kimbangu.

After the arrest and deportation of the prophet, the movement had continued to grow rapidly, and the Kimbanguist Church continued the pacifism as taught and lived by Simon Kimbangu. The Kimbanguist understanding of Christ is deeply liberating. But the authorities continued to fear the political consequences of a movement which practised human dignity so completely. The emphatic non-racism of the movement seemed to be a serious threat to colonial authority. Consequently, the movement was frequently and severely persecuted. In the early 1920's the early home of the movement, N'Kamba, was completely destroyed. During the early 1950's

37,000 Kimbanguist families were deported from their homes and resettled in strange new communities far from home. In 1956 the Protestant churches attempted to excommunicate all Kimbanguists, an action which quickly propelled this movement towards a denominational integrity of its own.[7]

In the Kinshasa area in 1956 the government took rather severe steps against the new denomination. But in spite of serious police harrassment and beatings the movement continued to grow. Hundreds of Kimbanguist young people poured through the streets of Kinshasa singing,

Go into the villages and proclaim salvation,
Everywhere on earth preach forgiveness to the oppressed!
Armed with the Gospel go from town to town,
Win the whole wide world for God !
Bear the message of hope to all sinners,
And preach Jesus Christ![8]

As the new denomination began to take shape, the harrassment and persecution became so intense that the leaders finally made a bold move. Six hundred leading residents of Kinshasa, who belonged to the Kimbanguist Church, signed a letter written to the Belgian Governor-General. The letter said, 'We are suffering so much. Wherever we meet for prayer, we are arrested by your soldiers. In order not to burden the police with added work, we shall all gather—unarmed—in the stadium, where you can arrest us all at once or massacre us.'[9] While the letter was being delivered, thousands of Kimbanguists throughout the city left their jobs and began preparations for converging peacefully on the stadium for arrest or death. Others were praying.

The Governor-General was stunned! Although he could not grant them official recognition, he did grant the Church of Jesus Christ on Earth through Simon Kimbangu, 'toleration.'[10] The political implications of granting toleration to the Kimbanguists were significant. This authentic grass roots ground swell of a people who were deeply committed to living redemptively and willing to suffer and die for their freedom in Christ, these remarkable Christians who lived the confrontational pacifism of the cross, were the forerunners of independence in Zaire.

It is astonishing that a young man from the tiny N'Kamba village, whose public ministry spanned hardly more than five months (and three of those months were in seclusion so as to avoid arrest), could affect Zaire so deeply. It is apparent that through the ministry of Simon Kimbangu, Jesus Christ became powerfully and attractively relevant in Zairean society. The Church of Jesus Christ on Earth through Simon Kimbangu perceives that their own redemption experience parallels with the history of salvation in the Bible, right from the Old Testament to the New Testament. Redemptive suffering is at the heart of their faith. Through the vulnerability of redemptive love a peoplehood is created who are truly and gloriously free.[11]

The Kimbanguist Church in Zaire today is one of the principal communities for reconciliation and unity in the nation.[12] Spiritual union with the widely scattered congregations is celebrated twice annually in pilgrimages to N'Kamba. These biannual meetings not only bring the widely scattered congregations together, they are an occasion for communion with one another, with those who have departed (especially with their spiritual leader, Simon Kimbangu), and with God in only whom we experience true fellowship.

The spirit of communion at the pilgrimages was dramatically demonstrated during the golden jubilee celebrations of the Church in April 1971. Three hundred and fifty thousand pilgrims came from all parts of Zaire to N'Kamba, and at that time the Kimbanguist Church celebrated its first Eucharist. The communion was shared on the golden (fiftieth) anniversary of the beginning of Simon Kimbangu's ministry in April, 1921. The communion elements consisted of food locally available; bread baked from a mixture of potatoes, maize and bananas, and wine made of honey and water. Sweet honey was used because, like the Holy Spirit, it gives instant strength and provides the resources needed for wholesome living. The bread was a sign of unity:

Just as the body which was given for us saves us, so maize and potatoes have saved millions in the world. Just as the ingredients maize, potatoes, and bananas are mixed, so the body of Christ is formed of men and women of all races and lands. Just as potatoes were formerly introduced from America and have now spread over almost the whole earth, so it is our task as the light of the world to proclaim to all peoples the Good News from Palestine. [13]

The coat of arms of this church is also replete with symbols and reconciliation: a red heart on a green background, intersected with a cross, sometimes entwined by a serpent, with open palm leaves beneath the cross. The meaning: the serpent is evil, the red heart symbolizes the blood shed on the cross which cleanses evil, the palm leaves, the victory over evil. The green is for hope. Other symbols include three doves as a sign of the union of the Trinity, and the unity of the three sons of Simon Kimbangu. The unity of the Trinity, expressed in the unity of the Church! One dove is a symbol of the Holy Spirit, through whom we experience peace. A star is often included with the cross. It reminds believers that Jesus Christ is their redemptive and reconciling star. [14]

The Church of Jesus Christ on Earth through Simon Kimbangu in Zaire began as a revival within the mission-planted churches, but then in the 1950's, as the movement matured, an independent church emerged which has taken on the characteristics of a denomination. Yet inspite of its denominational characteristics, this church which was formed through African initiatives, is a principal reconciling community in Zaire today.

The East African Revival Fellowship

In East Africa, the Revival Fellowship has become one of the principal integrative forces in the community, a fellowship of reconciliation which authentically transcends traditional social divisions. Admittedly the East Africa Revival Fellowship has had its schisms, and even violent aberrations. Yet the mainstream of the movement has been deeply reconciliatory. It is the fellowshipping, reconciling, mainstream of the movement which we are describing.

East African Christianity has been characterized by outbreaks of revival. Thus it is difficult to pinpoint the origin of the East African Revival Fellowship. Was it the 1893 revival which swept Buganda

124

after missionary George Pilkington experienced a deep renewal in the Holy Spirit which led him to confess wrong attitudes to his fellow missionaries and Africans? That child-like act of genuine repentance and reconciliation led to a mighty revival in Buganda and propelled the early Church outward in vigorous evangelistic outreach to the peoples north, south, east, and west of the Kingdom of Buganda. Or was it the charismatic renewal which swept the Kaimosi area of Kenya in 1927 following Arthur Chilson's call for genuine conversion?

It is probably inappropriate to pinpoint the historical beginning of the Revival Fellowship. East African revivalists say that it began at Calvary, when Jesus shed his blood for the forgiveness of sinners. Nevertheless, this movement of the Holy Spirit seems to have begun in a special way with the conversion of a Muganda teacher, Blasio Kigozi, who was teaching at a remote Church Missionary Society school far from home in Rwanda. He felt discouraged with his work and lukewarm about spiritual existence. So during a school term in 1935 he spent a week in his hut, praying and fasting. The Spirit of God touched him. He left his retreat and put things right with his family. He joined a small group of believers called the *abaka* (men of fire) because they preached and believed in being newly born.[15]

This small group of *abaka* seemed to threaten the staid churchly structures. So Blasio was brought before the Church Missionary Society (C.M.S.) council to be interrogated. Instead, the Holy Spirit fell on the entire council, and the meeting turned into an event of confession, repentance, renewal and reconciliation! All of the council became *abaka*.

The fire of revival swept across the countryside. There were pentecostal outbreaks. Astonished missionaries thought 'heathenism' had taken over the Church, yet the moral transformation of the revivalists was indisputable. Although Blasio died suddenly in 1936, his death became a mighty call for repentance in his homeland Church of Uganda. Through his death, Blasio, who had been a Muganda missionary to Rwanda, became a witness for revival in his own home community of Buganda in Uganda. Revival swept through the Church in Uganda. From there the movement spread east into Kenya and south into Tanganyika (Tanzania). [16]

The revival reached my home community in Tanzania in 1943. I was only a child, but I shall never forget the events of those days. In one of the Church centres a communion was scheduled. Christians had come from many miles around for the communion. Yet before the service the leaders sensed that there was sin within the congregation. For this reason during the communion service the leaders told the congregation that, because of sin within the fellowship, the Spirit of God had not given them freedom to serve the communion. That was mid-morning, Sunday. Thereafter, soul searching swept the congregation. Confession continued with tears until late Sunday night. One unrepentant woman ran from the church crying that stones were being thrown at her, so great was the crisis she was experiencing. Many from surrounding villages avoided coming near the Church centre for many days after the event, because they said the fire of God had descended on the Church.

In all of these revivalist movements confession of sin was a prominent aspect of the conversion experience, but the revival movement quickly became a sustaining fellowship at which brethren and sisters would meet to confess their sins before one another in the presence of the Lord, to meditate on the Scriptures, to share in the happenings which had taken place among the brotherhood, and then to celebrate in praise and worship the reality of forgiveness experienced through the shed blood of Christ, the Lamb of God. These were the dominant themes of fellowship meetings throughout East Africa: confession, experiencing forgiveness through the shed blood of the Lamb, followed by celebration and joy in the experience of a redeemed peoplehood.

The revivalists were a people who 'walked in the light' and who lived in 'brokenness' in their relationships with one another. They challenged one another to live in complete transparency and humility. They lived in the joy of precious fellowship. This fellowship is the only community in East Africa which authentically transcends ethnic, racial, denominational, economic, or national barriers. It really is a new people-hood.

LIVING IN PEACE

The East African Revivalist Movement has always been sustained by the small house-fellowship. These groups normally meet weekly, although they may meet more frequently too. Then on a regularly planned basis, the small house-fellowships congregate in a larger meeting for sharing with all the brotherhood within the area. And every several years there are conventions for brethren from all over East Africa. As many as 50,000 people have attended these large international gatherings of the 'saved ones' *(abalokole)*, as they are called. One of the truly remarkable aspects of the East African Revival Fellowship is that this sustaining and organized expression or renewal has remained mostly non-schismatic. The brethren are active members of the missionary-planted Churches in East Africa: Catholic, Baptist, Methodist, Presbyterian, Anglican, Pentecostal or Mennonite, as well as some of them belonging to the independent churches.

There have been a number of periods in modern East African history when the national or international situation has seriously distorted community relationships. One of the most obvious forms of distortion were white racism and the colonialist mentality. During the colonial heyday in East Africa some churches and clubs were not integrated. In Kenya, especially, vast areas of the best land were confiscated for white settlement. These tragic distortions of human rights and community threatened to destroy the very fabric of inter-racial working relationships. Yet the fellowship bound black people and white people together as brethren. Within the fellowship the races were united in a precious bond of unity.

MAU MAU

During Kenya's war for independence (Mau Mau) this bond of inter-racial unity was often a testimony to the kind of new community which a modern harmonious nation requires. It was at the height of the Mau Mau war that some European *abalokole* friends of mine travelled from Tanganyika, as it then was, to Kenya. They spent several days in coastal Mombasa, where they were strangers, but they did look up some of the *abalokole*. The word spread throughout

127

the brotherhood that several white brethren were in town. The visitors were taken to fellowship meetings and rejoiced over with hospitality and love. The African brethren even provided their transport during their time in Mombasa. And on departure day scores of *abalokole* brothers and sisters came to the train station to embrace and say a loving farewell to these brethren who had visited among them. As the train pulled out of the station, the *abalokole* filled the whole railroad station with songs of praise to the Lord who creates such precious fellowship. Other Europeans on the train, who knew nothing of the Revival Fellowship, and only knew of the horrors of the war for independence, could not believe their eyes or ears — how could Africans and Europeans love one another so deeply!

Mau Mau was a subtle challenge to the Church. The movement was committed to unity and freedom, goals which the Church as a whole believed in. Many Mau Mau leaders were sympathetic to the Gospel; most had studied in Church schools. Yet to the *abalokole* Christians especially, Mau Mau seemed a grievous distortion of their Christian commitment, and consequently they refused to join the Mau Mau.[17]

I have listened to *abalokole* sharing their experiences during Mau Mau. It seems that there are three main reasons why they refused to join the Mau Mau freedom fighters.

First, members of the movement required all participants to take an oath of unity. A second oath was for violence, binding people to fight for their country. Christian *abalokole* were especially scandalized that some of the oathing ritual seemed to deliberately imitate the sacrifice of Christ.[18] The oath included the sacrifice of a goat. It was a variation of the covenant sacrifice described in Chapter Three. Through the flesh and blood of the goat, the participants were united in an indissoluble community committed to justice and peace. The participants passed through an arch during the ceremony symbolizing the transition from disunity into ontocratic unity with one another and the ancestral living-dead, a unity which God the Life-Giver established. But for the Christian *abalokole* who had been united in covenant with God and with one another through the sacrificial death of the Lamb of God, it was impossible to eat or drink also of the blood or flesh of the goat of the oath. A Gikuyu pastor told me, 'We who had shared in the precious flesh and blood of the Lamb of God in the Holy Communion could never violate that blood by sharing in the flesh and blood of the Mau Mau oath'.

Another reason for refusing to take the Mau Mau oath was the movement's espousal of violence, which was directed against those who refused to take the oath as well as those who had seized the land of the Gikuyu. But the clear teaching of Christ is that those who take the sword will perish by the sword. As followers of Jesus, the *abalokole* refused to commit violence against their fellow human beings, even if they had done them wrong. They knew that violence breeds violence. Their only weapon was the weapon of love, of reconciling ministry. They shared the cup of cold water in the name of Christ with both the Mau Mau soldiers and the colonials.

Third, the blood of the Lamb of God was shed for all races and peoples. Because of Jesus, there is neither black nor white. Some of the Mau Mau freedom fighters were baptized Christians who had partaken of the blood of Christ in the Holy Communion. Some of the white colonial soldiers were also Christians. Both had partaken of that one cup of the blood of the covenant in the Christian eucharist. Thus the blood of the Lamb of God had sealed the black Christians and the white Christians together into an indissoluble unity and a precious, joyous brotherhood. How could one then shoot a covenant brother for whom Christ has died? How could one do violence against any one for whom Christ has died?

Many *abalokole* in central Kenya suffered greatly for their stand during the Mau Mau freedom war. The Late Rev. Heshbon Mwangi of Kahuhia bore facial scars from his experience, as described in the following biographical sketch.

Heshbon learned that the Mau Mau wanted to turn his school into a resistance school. Heshbon said, 'This is already a tribal school. Why should we change?'

One evening in 1952, after Heshbon had gone to bed, he heard somebody pound on his door with a corncutter knife. He shouted, 'Who's there?'

The answer was, 'Me'.

'Well, don't do that anymore!' Heshbon got up quickly and went to the door. He opened it, and the man ran away. A group of men were standing on the road. Nothing further happened that evening, but Heshbon was concerned because the wages for the six teachers of his school were in his house, in cash.

Next morning, with this money in a bag, Heshbon went to school on his bicycle. Groups of people stood along the road watching him and muttering. Heshbon didn't know that they had sent for the Mau Mau from the forest to attack him. When he reached the school, the teachers were standing in a group talking, the children were all lined up, ready for inspection.

He took money into the office, locked it up, and then came back out. 'All right, children,' he said, 'time for inspection.' Suddenly men ran in, grabbed Heshbon, overpowered him and began to beat him. The men had knives and pistols.

As they beat Heshbon they asked, 'Who is Jesus?'

He replied, 'Jesus is the Son of God and my Saviour.'

'Can't you say you are one of us?'

'No, I belong to Jesus.'

They continued to beat him mercilessly. 'Give us the money!'

'I have none here.'

Then they slashed his face. His blood flowed freely.

'Don't you know Jesus is a white man?......'

'No,' said Heshbon. 'He is the Son of God.'

'Jesus is an Asian.'

'No. He is the Son of God and my Saviour. He will be yours too if you receive him.'

'Kill him!' shouted one. 'Shoot him,' yelled another.

Heshbon said, 'Wait a bit. I have nothing against you. Only that I love Jesus.'

The teachers had been threatened and they just stood there. Pupils were crying, and running away. They loved their teacher, and they thought he would surely die.

The men searched him for money. They found none, but they found his Bible.

'What's this Book?'

'That's Jesus' Book.'

Then they knocked out his front teeth, upper and lower.

One attacker said, 'Let's not kill him. Let him teach the children.' And miraculously the men began to leave him, some to look for the money. From the ground Heshbon called, 'I forgive you for my blood and for my teeth. I forgive you, and I will pray for you!'

One came back and trampled on him, but another said, 'Let him go on teaching the children.'

They broke into the office, took the money, and left.

At last Heshbon was all alone. He was badly hurt. After some time, he tried to stand up. The pupils had run through town spreading the news that their teacher had been killed. The rest of the teachers were stunned and didn't move to help. Slowly Heshbon walked to the local dispensary, but they couldn't do much for him.

Heshbon started for home. He was greatly relieved when he was met by two brothers who had come on their bicycles as fast as they could from Weithaga. Having heard that he was dead, they had come to pick up his body for burial.

When they saw him, they said, 'Brother! You are alive!'

And he said, 'I have Jesus'.

There are many similar stories of suffering and martyrdom coming out of the Mau Mau freedom struggle. Often the *abalokole* were arrested and imprisoned by the colonial authorities because their peace witness seemed treasonable. Similarly the Mau Mau persecuted many of these Christians who refused to engage in the war against colonialism. Hundreds, perhaps thousands, died. Whenever a Christian was slain, if it was possible, brothers and sisters from miles around came to the funeral in buses, trucks, bicycles, or on foot, and as they travelled they filled the countryside with songs of praise to the Lamb of God. They rejoiced that another member of the fellowship was counted worthy to be a martyr of the Lamb. Consequently, in Kenya the *abalokole* earned a new name for themselves: The People of the Lamb.[20]

The *abalokole* spoke much about repentance from all forms of hate, bitterness, or a non-forgiving spirit. In continuity with the insights of their African traditional heritage and Biblical revelation, they sought to prevent any forms of hate from eating into the fellowship. Love for the Mau Mau and love for the colonialists was taught and practised. Both the colonialists and the Mau Mau were offered the 'cup of water' in the name of Jesus.

One of the brethren told me of his testimony to a white officer who tried to get him to carry a gun in self-defence. He told the officer of the love of Jesus, and assured him that his only weapon was the love of God revealed at Calvary. As he shared his testimony, the officer began to weep tears. That was the witness of these brethren during those dreadful days of death and terror in central Kenya.

Today many of the former Mau Mau have been converted and are themselves *abalokole*. I have frequently heard the testimony in Kenya, 'I used to be a member of the Mau Mau, but the love of God finally captured me'. The love of God not only captured freedom fighters; it also captured some of the colonialists.[21] Certainly the reconciling love expressed by the *abalokole* did much to help heal the bitterness of the war, and contributed to the reconciliatory spirit which has blessed Kenya's independent nationhood.[22]

At Murang'a in the central highlands of Kenya a cathedral has been erected which is called the Church of the Martyrs. It was built in memory of those whose reconciliatory testimony became a witness unto death. No names are inscribed on the walls of the cathedral. Instead the walls portray murals of the life of Jesus in a Gikuyu setting by Elimo Njau: birth, baptism, last supper, Gethsemane, and Calvary. The violence of the Mau Mau war against colonialism lurks darkly in the background; thatched houses are burning, and the skeletons of death are there. But death does not have the final word. The thread which binds those murals together is not death; it is the life-giving blood which flows from the crucified Christ. A stream of crimson is the uniting thread which binds all the murals together; the way of the blood flows from Calvary in the last mural to the manger cradle of the first. The murals suggest that it is the blood of the crucified Lamb of God which gives coherence to his entire life and mission; the sacrifice on Calvary gives cohesion.

harmony, unity, victory and life, even in the midst of violence. In his crucifixion, violence and death have lost their power.

There are several gates leading into the church yard. They are called reconciliation gates. The iron work in the gates is a revelation of the peace theology of the *abalokole*. The cross is central. A Mau Mau sword stands on one side of the cross. A colonial gun is on the other side. The sword and gun are tilted, so that they both meet at the base of the cross. This is a sign that when enemies humble themselves under the Lordship of the Lamb and meet as sinners beneath his cross where the blood can flow over them, thereby cleansing their bitterness and hate, then those who used to carry weapons against one another are united. All the weapons of destruction are rendered impotent at the foot of the cross!

Above the cross is a dove, the dove of peace, who is the Spirit of God. When enemies are reconciled through the cleansing blood of Jesus, then there is genuine peace. The dove of peace descends upon those who are reconciled.

In order to experience peace and reconciliation, one passes through a gate. Among the Samburu the weapons of war were broken and formed a gate through which the reconciling parties passed, similarly new Mau Mau recruits went through an arch of unity. In Christian experience one needs to go through the gate of reconciliation to become a newly redeemed person. That is God's invitation to everyone. At the Church of the Martyrs in central Kenya the worshippers pass through those gates of reconciliation week after week as they congregate together for worship. The gates are a reminder that through Christ's sacrificial death on the cross our former enemies can experience profound and miraculous reconciliation, a healing of relationships which creates a new people.

In 1969, only six years after Kenya achieved independence, there was a renewal of oathing for unity in central Kenya. This developed out of the political crisis surrounding the assassination of Tom Mboya, a prominent politician. The oathing represented ethnic sectarianism. Multitudes of Christians in central Kenya refused to have anything to do with the renewed oathings. A number of Church leaders were martyred for their stand. The Church throughout Kenya cried out against what was happening. A massive meeting of thousands of *abalokole* from all parts of the Republic came together in central Kenya for a mighty testimony to the nation of their unity in Christ and their unequivocal stand against the forces of division or prejudice. During the 1969 crisis the unity in Christ of these *abalokole* was a powerful leaven for unity within the Kenyan nation as a whole.[23]

The East African Revival Fellowship has also given a witness for reconciliation and peace in other situations. We cannot discuss all the dimensions of this ministry of reconciliation. Two additional comments will suffice: the Rwanda massacres of the late 1950s and early 1960s and the witness of the Church in Uganda during the rule of Idi Amin from 1971 to 1979.

Rwanda

We have mentioned that the East African Revival Fellowship originated in Rwanda during the 1930s. In the late 1950s violence exploded throughout Rwanda between the ruling class of Tutsi and the Hutu agriculturists; the latter comprised the larger portion of the population. For centuries the Tutsi had been the rulers, but the disaffected Hutu were bent on revolution. Massacres and pillaging swept the land.

During the height of the crisis *abalokole* from other East African countries wrote letters to the Rwanda brethren urging them to live in reconciliation. Rev. Heshbon Mwangi, who we have mentioned in connection with the violence during Mau Mau in Kenya, sent this word to the Rwanda brethren, 'Keep a positive testimony, both in word and deed. Use only one weapon—that of Calvary's love for all, particularly those who are persecuting you.'[24] Only one weapon: love!

Those several years of violence in Rwanda are replete with heroic incidents of Hutu attempting to protect Tutsi brethren from the violence of the revolution, or of Tutsi protecting Hutu from counter-revolutionary violence. The power of reconciling love affected the countryside. Those who loved were often respected, and their lives spared. The Church opened refugee centres in various places, some of which were called 'praise the Lord', by the revolutionaries because of the songs of praise which they could hear. They rarely attacked such centres.[25]

These refugee centres were open to anyone. Tutsi and Hutu crowded together. Remarkably, they lived in peace. At one centre the refugees would reprimand anyone who started a quarrel by saying, 'You must not talk like that on God's hill'.[26] The *abalokole* sometimes referred to themselves as 'the Party of Jesus'.[27] They were a new community who did not recognize tribal loyalty as being of ultimate concern. They stood under the 'power hierarchy' of Christ who is Lord of both the Tutsi and Hutu. They were a new community in Christ. They were a reconciled and joyous peoplehood and were therefore the only community in Rwanda able to bridge the chasm between the two opposing sides.

The brethren forgave their enemies. All forms of bitterness and unforgiving spirit were judged as unworthy of the people of the Lamb. Often the communion service became a time for confession of unforgiving attitudes towards those who had killed or destroyed. Only the forgiven and the forgiving were worthy to eat at the table of the Lord. The cup of the new covenant could not be shared when one was not living in new covenant relationships. The communion service was a sign of a profound experience of reconciliation and peace.[28]

Even in death the witness to the love of God was given. Rwandans tell the story of a senior headmaster who was beaten and then shot to death. As he was dying, he cried out, 'I have done nothing wrong. I am not in any party because I am a saved man. I do not hate anybody. I am not afraid to die for I shall go to my Heavenly Home.'[29]

Twenty years later Rwanda again plunged into the abyss of Hutu-Tutsi conflict. April 6, 1994, a suspicious plane crash killed the head of state, Juvenal Habyarimana. That tragedy was the trigger for the massacres that followed.

It seems that those committed to violence chose to first attack the Revivalists *(abalokole)* who were known everywhere as the reconcilers. The day after the plane crash Israel Havigumana and two daughters were slain. He was the leader of Africa Enterprise, an *abalokole* movement specifically working in reconciliation between Tutsi and Hutu. His Africa Enterprise colleague, Bishop Donald Jacobs, estimates 50,000 other *abalokole* were killed in the massacres that followed.

However, the universal witness is that in the midst of this horrible violence the *abalokole* stood firm even in death. They did not and would not hate or kill. They were the People of the Lamb, Jesus, who even in his crucifixion, forgave his enemies. The witness of these Christians who have lived and proclaimed forgiveness and reconciliation in Jesus Christ has been an authentic witness to the Rwandan people that the Way of Jesus is the only real hope for the healing of their nation.

UGANDA

In 1971 Idi Amin took power in nearby Uganda. Just as in Rwanda, ethnic divisions threatened to totally destroy the fabric of Ugandan society. The ethnic animosities were sometimes fuelled by religious divisions. To a certain extent the Ugandan tragedy represented Muslim-Christian tension.

During the early part of Idi Amin's reign, especially as atrocities began to multiply, a few of the *abalokole* churchmen approached the President urging restraint. They tried to give a quiet, unpublicized witness of reconciliation in the highest echelons of Ugandan government. Yet as political developments unfolded, the hierarchical nature of Amin's political structure became increasingly autocratic as he attempted to secure his position and power.

One of the first indications of things to come is described by Bishop Festo Kivengere.

> In the summer of 1972 an all-East-African convention of the 'revival brethren' was planned to be held in Tanzania. These are great times of getting together—5,000, 10,000 or 25,000 people attend—and have been held in different places every year or two since about 1940. It is a wonderful thing to praise God with so many brothers and sisters and to listen to what God is saying to us in today's circumstances.

136

On the day of departure a chartered bus was at the terminal, being loaded with the Ugandan delegation to the convention. Because of the political strain between our country and Tanzania, each one had carefully gotten a permit from the Department of Military Affairs for this trip.

A crowd came down to see the travellers off. They were singing, laughing, hugging, and waving. Suddenly, up drove some army officers and a detachment of soldiers with guns and loud commands. They surrounded the whole group, delegates and friends, and marched them off to the dreaded military prison. About eighty people were jailed.

Someone had whispered a question in a high place about a large group going to the 'enemy' country of Tanzania. Were they planning to join the guerillas there? Prison was the answer.

The Christians filed into the central cell of the prison in shock. There were no chairs to sit on, so in the usual Ugandan style they spread out their grass mats, with which they travel, and sat on the floor. Over in one corner someone began to sing softly: 'Glory, glory, hallelujah, glory to the Lamb . . .' Everyone picked it up, and in that moment they began to repent of their fear for their lives. The praise swelled and rolled through the corridors of the most terrifying jail of Uganda, while tears of joy and release shone in the eyes of many.

Many quietly shared the change that had come to their hearts as Jesus spoke peace to them. Each one praised God.

'We thought we were going to a convention in Tanzania,' said one. 'But we are having a convention right here!'

For two days the soldiers were exposed to the most joyous atmosphere they had ever experienced: men and women praising God that they were in prison, sharing their testimonies and the Scriptures with the soldiers, who felt loved. The soldiers' wives started slipping in to listen in amazement, too.

Some soldiers went out to buy soft drinks for their new friends! A number of them felt convicted by sin and asked how they could know this Jesus, too.

Outside, the archbishop and others were busy visiting offices, explaining and showing the travel permits to the top military men and to the President, whom they finally convinced that these were loyal citizens and the trip was perfectly in order. The command was given to release them.

The soldiers and their wives lined up to shake hands with the Christians as they filed out, and they have never forgotten the love and the free spirit of these people, who knew they could lose their lives there. In fact, that year very few who had entered that prison walked out. Most had been buried.[30]

The event which finally shook the Christian world happened five years later. On the night of 8 February, 1977, security police forcefully entered the home of Archbishop of the Church of Uganda, Rwanda, Burundi, and Boga-Zaire at Namirembe, Kampala. At gun point they forced Archbishop Janani Luwum to permit them to search his home. The bishops of the Church felt that this incident dramatically demonstrated that a gun was being 'pointed at every Christian in the Church....'[31]

The bishops, most if not all of whom were *abalokole*, met in a solemn assembly at Namirembe to consider appropriate action. They wrote a letter to the President lamenting the breakdown in communication between the government and the Church, and urged that steps be taken to end terrorism and recreate a spirit of reconciliation. They deplored that, 'the gun which was meant to protect Uganda as a nation, the Ugandan as a citizen, and his property is increasingly being used against the Ugandan to take away his life and his property'.[32] The letter concluded by pointing out that the Church of Uganda was part of a worldwide fellowship of believers, a community of faith which transcends not only ethnic barriers, but also international boundaries.[33]

Six days after the writing of that letter, Archbishop Janani Luwum was martyred. He knew that martyrdom was likely as he led the bishops through those days of painful decision concerning what steps the Church should take in the crisis gripping Uganda. He knew that the Church was called by God to confront injustice in the Spirit of love. He knew that in confrontation there would be suffering.[34]

Yet even in the suffering, the Church was triumphant. Eye witnesses said that the Archbishop died while praying aloud for his captors and fellow martyrs! The memorial service at Namirembe Cathedral on Sunday, 20 February, was a great testimony of joy and victory. The favourite song of the *abalokole,* 'Glory, glory to the Lamb', engulfed Namirembe hill.[35]

Immediately after the overthrow of the Idi Amin regime in 1979, the provisional government of Uganda urged the Church to become involved in a ministry of reconciliation throughout the nation. There was a recognition that without forgiveness, bitterness would feed the fires of revenge, and Uganda would be further fragmentized. In that crisis the Gospel of reconciliation, for which Archbishop had given his life, was recognized as one of the most precious gifts of the Church to the reconstruction process.

A Comparison of Kimbanguism and the Revival Fellowship

Neither the Kimbanguist movement in Zaire nor the Revival Fellowship in East Africa were initiated by missionaries. In fact, both movements experienced considerable missionary disfavour, at least during the early phases. In East Africa only the Mennonite Mission gave official endorsement to the Revival,[36] possibly because of the Revival Fellowship's apparent affinities with Anabaptism, particularly in its emphasis on the Church as being a redeemed and reconciled community of believers. Both Kimbanguism and Revival are authentic African responses to the Gospel. Both perceive the Gospel as being the creator of a new community of reconciliation.

Among the Kimbanguists, the new community receives its cohesive and reconciling power by participating in an eponymal hierarchy: The Church of Jesus Christ on Earth through Simon Kimbangu. The prophet, like Christ, became authentically authoritative through his ministry of service. Because he loved even his enemies, the prophet has been exalted and has become, as it were, the eponymal authority which holds the entire community together. This power to bind has been perpetuated through his sons who continue the ministry of prophetic leadership which their father began. Unity is further promoted by the pilgrimages to the shrine at N'Kamba, the New Jerusalem in which the prophet ministered and suffered.[37]

Because of suffering, the hierarchical nature of the Church of Jesus Christ on Earth through Simon Kimbangu has been made acceptable; the prophet has become the nodal point of harmony out of which the community experience reconciliation and life. There is harmony and life because Jesus is Lord and Simon Kimbangu is his prophet. The Kimbanguist Church is an interpretation of the Gospel in the light of traditional perception. It assumes a hierachical structure. It is not surprising, therefore, that such an interpretation would soon lead to a denomination in its own right. The Kimbanguist hierarchy was especially incompatible with papal authority, and it is probably for this reason the movement was especially threatening to Catholic sensibilities.[38]

In contrast to the Kimbanguist Church, the East African Revival Fellowship has emphasized blood sacrifice as being the central theme in the reconciliatory process. In both movements Christ as the Suffering Servant is centrally present. But in East Africa the Suffering Servant sheds his blood, and through his sacrifice we are forgiven and become blood brothers and sisters. These East African 'saved ones' are the People of the Lamb. It is through sacrifice, rather than through authenticated hierarchy, that the unity of the community is created and preserved. The sacrificial theme of the East African Revival makes unity mandatory with all who are cleansed by the blood of the Lamb, and therefore the movement has not been schismatic. Except for a few exceptions, the movement has flourished within the traditional Church structures.

In their respective ways (Christ as the epitome of power in Kimbanguism or Christ as the perfect sacrifice in the Revival Fellowship), both movements are deeply meaningful African interpretations of the Gospel. And in both, suffering love redeems and recreates an authentic, joyous, reconciling and life-enhancing community.

The Church of Jesus Christ on Earth through Simon Kimbangu and the East African Revival Fellowship are rather spectacular examples of the breakthrough of the Gospel into traditional culture, with a subsequent interpretation of the Good News by that culture in a manner which is joyously relevant. Both these movements permeated their respective societies on the inner proppings of their traditional cultures.

The All Africa Conference of Churches (AACC)

There is another aspect of reconciliation which also needs to be mentioned. This has been given expression by large-scale organizations which are either affiliated or associated with even larger international organizations. At the level of international churchmanship in Africa, there are examples replete with reconciliation, as the following examples demonstrate.

SUDAN

One of the most noteworthy examples of the Church as a recognized international community giving leadership to reconciliation is the 1972 Sudan peace accords, which brought sixteen year respite after seventeen years of strife and civil war. (Tragically the civil war resumed again in 1988). Even before independence in 1956 tension between southern and northern Sudan erupted into isolated violence. Ethnic, economic and religious issues were at stake; the north was Arabized and Islamic, while the south was primarily Christian and traditionalist. After independence the northerners began pressing for the Islamization of the south. A primary instrument for Islamization was the introduction of Arabic into southern schools. The Christian and traditionalist south resented these pressures, and full-scale civil war developed. The southern freedom fighters organized themselves into a guerilla army called the Anya Nya. In retaliation the northern troops burnt churches and schools to the ground. All missionaries were expelled, and some Church leaders killed. Hundreds of thousands of Sudanese refugees fled south into Uganda and Zaire.[39]

Very early in the conflict the All Africa Conference of Churches attempted to mediate a settlement. In 1966 a delegation of the AACC was invited to Sudan to investigate the situation and make recommendations. This was in itself a most hopeful sign, as it showed the Sudan government's approval of the Church to be involved in mediation, which was extremely remarkable of a mainly Muslim government.[40]

Following the 1966 visit, the AACC continued its efforts at reconciliation. But it was not until early in 1972 that these attempts to mediate peace were finally successful. After extensive preliminary groundwork, official talks commenced in Addis Ababa between representatives of the Government of Sudan and the Southern Sudan Liberation Movement (SSLM). The consultation proceeded under the moderation of the General Secretary of the All Africa Conference of Churches in the presence of representatives of the Sudan Council of Churches and the World Council of Churches. The final agreement granted regional self government in the south and religious freedom to all Sudanese. The document was initialled by the Foreign Minister of the Sudan, Dr. Mansour Khalid, and the President of the SSLM. Major General Joseph Lagu, in the presence of Emperor Haile Selassie of Ethiopia.[41]

This agreement was a hoped for step forward in Christian-Muslim relations in the African continent. The spirit of the agreement was revealed in a reconciliation event which took place in Khartoum, the capital of Sudan, on Easter Sunday. The Secretary General of the AACC describes that joyous experience.

The Government of the Sudan and the SSLM had been locked in a campaign of hatred, bitterness, prejudices and fears that had destroyed the lives and property of hundreds of thousands of their people, impoverished their nation, and demoralised the entire continent of Africa. After many years of patient and quiet efforts, the Church of Jesus Christ had been used by God to bring the two peoples together in order to search for a peaceful settlement to the forgotten war across the 'grass curtain'. Two weeks of hard negotiations had produced a settlement, initialled and later ratified in Addis Ababa, the capital of Ethiopia, Africa's most ancient Christian land.

Yet questions lingered. Was the reconciliation complete? Should General Lagu travel to Khartoum? Would he be safe there? How would the hunted be received by the hunter?

All scepticism at once evaporated in the jubilant welcome that awaited our party, comprising the representatives of the Government of Sudan and leaders of the South Sudan Liberation Movement, at Khartoum Airport.

There were old friends and comrades-in-arms who had not seen one another for eight years; some for twelve years; others for twenty years. There were Anya Nya soldiers who had never once set foot in Khartoum. All were heartily and warmly welcome! The atmosphere of national relief was transparent and genuine in the faces of every man on the street.

That was on holy Saturday. Animosity and bitterness were buried with Jesus in the grave. The next day, Easter Day, a new spirit of total and complete reconciliation was to be born when President Numeiry and General Lagu embraced each other. A new hope for peace with justice, dignity and mutual respect was unleashed. An embittered people would get a new lease of life. Magnanimity would be the order of the day.

Those of us who represented the Church watched and remembered the words of Jeremiah, 'I will forgive them their iniquity and I will remember their sin no more'. We experienced the reality of Easter in a manner we had never done before. We were humbled by the thought that we had been permitted to be enablers of this act of reconciliation. We felt moved by the power of Paul's central theme, 'this Jesus we speak of has been raised by God, as we can all bear witness.' Yes, we did indeed witness the power of the resurrection reconciling men of different ethnic, cultural and even religious traditions. We came away filled with hope and reassured that the power of the Resurrected Lord is still at work in Africa today.[42]

The AACC and other Christian communities recognized that genuine justice, peace and reconciliation had to go beyond a euphoric embrace on Easter Sunday. Immediately following the peace accords, the churches united in a massive reconstruction effort throughout Southern Sudan. The worldwide Church was invited to participate in 'building' the peace. Along with the reconstruction aid the churches also became engaged in vigorous evangelistic effort.

Tens of thousands of people were brought into the Church as the meaning of the reconciliation process gained root throughout the bushlands of Southern Sudan.

However, there is a tragic dimension to the Sudan peace. Peace-making is not a once and done affair. We must continually work together to build the peace. Somehow as the 1980's progressed peace in Sudan came under increasing stress. International developments such as the alienation of Libya and Iran from other nations in the Middle East and global arena contributed to the fracturing of the peace in Sudan. Both Christians and Muslims in Sudan did not keep working hard enough together to network for peace; consequently militant Islam with strong outside support overwhelmed the political processes. By 1988 Sudan had regressed again into civil war.

SOUTHERN AFRICA

Sudan represents a Muslim-Christian conflict with Church involvement in reconciliation. Southern Africa has been a different kind of challenge, because the racism of some of the churches of Southern Africa meant that the struggle for liberation and justice in that part of the continent has been in a special way a conflict between Christians. There have been, of course, many noble examples of Christians, both black and white, who have committed themselves to justice and reconciliation in southern Africa. Many have suffered deeply for their commitment to justice and reconciliation: Nelson Mandela, Steve Biko, Chief Albert Luthuli, Alan Paton, David Bosch, Manas Buthelezi, Allen Boesak, Desmond Tutu, Willie Silliers, John Degruchy, Janet Mondlane and John Rees. There are multitudes of others, too, who are hardly noticed, but who have serious commitment to the healing of brokenness in Southern Africa. Each represents a significant and beautiful story.

In South Africa multitudes of Christians chose the way of nonviolent prayerful confrontation with evil. It was a painful struggle, and many laid down their lives in the nonviolent struggle for justice, reconciliation, and peace. The conscience of the world community of nations was awakened by the struggle; South African athletes were not permitted to play in international competitions and for several years an economic boycott was imposed. During these years of struggle two South Africans were awarded the Nobel Peace Prize as a statement of global appreciation and affirmation for those who choose the way of nonviolent confrontation in the struggle for justice: Chief Albert J. Luthuli (1960) and Bishop Desmond Tutu (1984).

One of the most difficult issues facing the All Africa Conference of Churches in the 1970's and 80's was the structural and racist injustice in Southern Africa. Certainly, if ever there was a case for the Church condoning a 'just war', the freedom struggle in Southern Africa passed the test.[43] At the AACC quinquennium in 1974 held in Lusaka, Zambia, the issue of a just war was thoroughly debated. It was at that meeting that Canon Burgess Carr, then General Secretary of the AACC, presented his famous call for the Church's endorsement of selective 'violence'[44] to end injustice in Southern Africa. In his oratorial style he proclaimed that 'God in Jesus Christ, sanctified violence into a redemptive instrument....'[45]

The issue, both in its theological and practical implications, became the single most important agenda item in that meeting. President Kenneth Kaunda of Zambia had set the tone for the question in his opening address when he lamented that some white people falsely posing as Christian prophets had come to Africa with a gun in one hand and a Bible in the other. These people were responsible for intense human suffering, but their structures of injustice would soon collapse for they were morally bankrupt. He strongly endorsed the Liberation Movements which 'are helping to create conditions in which the aspirations expressed in the Christian Gospel can be fulfilled'.[46] With tears on his face the President of Zambia urged the Church to continue 'carrying the banner of human rights very high.... '[47]

President Kaunda's tears dramatized the agony of that assembly as it contemplated Southern Africa. Should the Church endorse the use of the gun in the struggle for justice? Pragmatically the answer seemed to be 'yes'. But was 'yes' the answer of the Lord of the Church who breaks the powers of injustice and death through suffering redemptive love as revealed in the cross?

Has the cross really sanctified violence? Should the Church endorse all means possible to bring justice, or should the Church use only the weapons of love to bring both justice and reconciliation? These issues were debated intensely in the corridors and in the main assembly at Lusaka. When the final vote came, the resolution which would have tacitly endorsed violence for justice was narrowly defeated. The Assembly went on record as supporting reconciliation.[48]

Although the AACC General Assembly did not explicitly condone violence in the quest for justice, we need to recognize that some African churchmen do espouse a theology which does condone the 'just war' when all other attempts in the quest for justice have failed. This is the position of Bishop Abel Muzorewa who in 1971 became President of the African National Council (ANC), a political grouping in Rhodesia committed to the liberation struggle. The good Bishop describes his pilgrimage, a spiritual movement which in some ways resembles that of Dietrich Bonhoeffer during the Nazi regime in Germany. Both men were deeply committed to non-violence at the beginning. Yet eventually they condoned violence as what seemed to them to be the only way of dealing with the cancer which was destroying their respective societies.

The Bishop points out that the ANC came about because of the Church's anxiety to deal with justice in Southern Africa in a non-violent manner, in the hope of achieving authentic reconciliation. But the racist regimes would not listen to reason. (He compares the Smith regime in Rhodesia to a 'mad man' who enters one's home to kill and rob.) After four years of fruitless efforts at negotiating with the racist powers in Rhodesia, the ANC finally felt compelled to condone violence. This was a last resort, but even then the armed struggle was seen in terms of a passing measure, a prelude to the evolvement of a more harmonious community in Rhodesia, as Zimbabwe was then called. It was not an anti-white, but an anti-injustice, anti-dehumanization, movement. And Bishop Muzorewa seems to have felt justified in his dual position as both a churchman and a leader of an armed freedom movement in Rhodesia.[49]

Bishop Muzorewa's position is not surprising or new, as there is a lot of evidence of theologians who throughout the centuries have defined and justified certain forms of violence. However, such a viewpoint is not shared by all African churchmen, as was indicated by the Archbishop of the Church of the Province of Kenya in his interview at the Nairobi airport on his return from the 1978 Lambeth Conference held at Canterbury. In the interview with the press, the Archbishop confessed he did not believe that the Church should condone violence as an instrument in the quest for justice. That, to him, was contrary to the Gospel which the Church proclaims!

The South African delegation to the third assembly of the All Africa Conference of Churches was impressed by the theological sensitivities of that meeting. They recognized that although the AACC did not overtly endorse violence for justice, the churches in South Africa, by supporting the racist regime, were involved in violence to perpetuate injustice. A principal function of the army and police force in South Africa was the enforcement of unjust structural violence. How could the Church in South Africa condone participation in a military machine bent on perpetuating injustice when the black churches of Africa as a whole were calling for justice and reconciliation in Southern Africa?

The South Africa Council of Churches (SACC) came to perceive that there were serious theological and moral problems in continuing to condone structural violence in South Africa. The agony of the issue finally led the SACC to call on all Christians in South Africa to seriously consider becoming conscientious objectors to any participation in the South Africa military. It called on Christians to desist from involvement in the instrument of structural violence in South Africa.[50] This statement by the South African Council of Churches angered the government, and for over a decade any discussion on the position of conscientious objectors in South Africa was punishable by very severe prison sentences and fines. This did not stop some white South Africans becoming conscientious objectors with regard to military service, but they suffered for their stand.

At another level there have been several regional or panAfrican conferences for renewal. These fellowship assemblies of Christian leaders in Africa during the 1970s dealt quite specifically with the issues of racism in southern Africa. Three of these conferences deserve special mention.

The first such conference was held in Johannesburg in 1973. Seven hundred people attended. It was the first inter-racial conference in South Africa since the apartheid system began to divide people into racial groups. It was therefore a momentous event, and was widely reported in the South African press. Blacks, coloureds and whites ate, slept and worshipped together in a mighty testimony to the reconciling power of the Gospel. Catholic, Protestant, and Independent church leaders participated together in this great festival of unity in Christ.

Then came the Pan African Christian Leadership Assembly held in Nairobi, Kenya in December 1976. This was a continental conference convened in the interest of evangelism. But the agenda became primarily southern Africa. The South African delegation entered the conference badly divided along racial lines. But in the process of the meeting, much reconciliation took place as the two groups learned to know one another as brothers and sisters in Christ. A great healing was experienced among them and they were determined to return to South Africa with this new message.[51]

As a further witness to what God had begun to do in Johannesburg in 1973 and then in Nairobi in 1976, Christian leaders in South Africa began preparations for a South African Christian Leadership Assembly to be held in Pretoria, the capital of the Republic of South Africa, and the heartland of Afrikaaner society. That assembly took place in July 1979.

Seven thousand Christian leaders from homes in Pretoria opened their doors to host black conference participants! Although the Dutch Reformed Church disassociated itself from the conference, ninety pastors and hundreds of lay leaders from that Church participated. For eleven days the races of South Africa intermingled together in fellowship and worship. They cried together and repented together. And they left that conference determined to continue to work together to transform the South African society to the glory of God.

One of the participants wrote, 'The Assembly did not adopt resolutions or issue statements. Rather the result of SACLA was the encouragement of ongoing, intense fellowship clusters in Christ throughout the land, a network of "in between" fellowships in which a variety of persons from the various races and denominations would commit themselves anew to Christ and one another. In this way, as social change occurs in the nation, as apartheid loses its grip, a new community of faith will be there to show the way. There was a clear call to count the cost of suffering.'[52]

These forms of high profile witness to reconciliation hit the front pages of newspapers. They were significant. Nevertheless, it is especially important to recognize that a meeting such as SACLA could never have happened unless there were hundreds of small cluster fellowships already living in reconciliation within the South African society. These small clusters of reconciling, transforming love were authentic leaven. In faith they anticipated becoming the models for justice and healing as the tragic disharmonies of the South African apartheid system crumbled. This is what happened in Zimbabwe. While the freedom war raged in the land which had been known as Rhodesia, clusters of black and white Christians began to discover one another as brothers and sisters in Christ. These joyous fellowships of reconciliation were a small light, a model of reconstructed community. As black majority rule is now a reality in Zimbabwe, those models of a new community have set the tone for the reconstruction and reconciliation process.

In South Africa, likewise, reconciliation fellowships laid the foundations for the astonishing transitions from apartheid. There were many such expressions of commitment to reconciliation. I shall detail briefly only one of those small threads of reconciliation that was linked to the *abalokole* of East Africa and the Africa Enterprise team. I have heard these reports from persons involved in the ministries of Africa Enterprise.

In 1992 forty East African brothers and sisters were hosted by their South African partners in fellowship. The East African team were called: From Africa with Love. These guests from outside the South African system in partnership with their South African hosts networked with South African political decision makers, of every persuasion from the communists to right wing Afrikaners. They prayed with each political leader whom they met, and through these relationships trust developed.

During the later part of 1992 and 1993 as the nation moved fearfully and with isolated incidents of violence toward the 1994 elections, these unobtrusive Christian reconcilers invited small clusters of twelve to twenty political leaders to desert retreats. They had six retreats hosting 90 key leaders. The participants in each of these retreats included the spectrum of South African political opinion and background.

Each retreat included fun things like going to a game park; the retreats also included prayer, reflections from the Bible, and the invitation to each participant to tell his or her personal story and dream for South Africa. For example, one man, a communist, shared that when in prison on Robben Island he had been buried in sand up to his neck, and then his captors urinated on his head and face. That account helped the Afrikaners understand why this man had sought to end the injustice of the system through the violence of a communist revolution. These retreats bonded these diverse political leaders into a fraternity of respect for one another.

However, as the April, 1994, elections drew near the largely Zulu Inkatha Freedom Party led by Chief Buthelezi were nonparticipants. Zulu Natal was on the edge of violent catalysm that threatened to pull the whole nation into an unimaginably horrible civil war. About a fortnight before the elections Henry Kissinger, Lord Carrington and other renowned international diplomats came to South Africa to explore ways through the impasse. They were utterly frustrated, and in despair returned home.

Nevertheless, behind the scenes one of the East African brethren was quietly at work. He was Professor Washington Okumu of Kenya who shuttled back and forth between the various protagonists while multitudes were in prayer. The breakthrough occurred on April 17. Thirty thousand people were gathered in Durban at King's Cross stadium for a prayer meeting for peace in South Africa. In the VIP lounge off stage a small group of key Inkatha, African National

Congress, government, and other political leaders met trying to find a way through the impasse while these 30,000 people were gathered in prayer for them. The Spirit of Jesus touched that group, for that day a dramatic transformation happened within those leaders. Inkatha joined in the elections.

I listened to B.B.C. news as the April 26-29 elections got underway. A commentator exclaimed, 'Miracle is the only way to express what has happened!' The South African *Daily News* ran a news feature captioned, 'The Day God stepped in to save South Africa.'

Conclusion

The mystery—the marvel of the redeemed, reconciling peoplehood who are the Church!

In the words of the Apostle Paul, 'All this is from God, who reconciled us to himself through Christ and gave us the ministry of reconciliation.' (II Cor 5: 18).

REFERENCES

1. Monica Wilson, *Religion and the Transformation of Society: A Study in Social Change in Africa*, Cambridge, Cambridge University Press, 1971.

2. Marie-Louise Martin, translated by D. M. Moore, *Kimbangu, An Afri can Prophet and His Church*, Grand Rapids, Eerdmans, 1976, 146.

3. Ibid., 38.

4. Ibid., 60.

5. Ibid, 60-63.

6. Ibid., 63.

7. Ibid., 104.

8. Ibid., 105.

9. Ibid., 106.

10. Ibid., 106.

11. Ibid., 154-6.

12. Ibid., 128.

13. Ibid., 181.

14. Ibid., 156-7.

15. W.B. Anderson, *The Church in East Africa, 1840-1974*, Dodoma, Central Tanganyika Press, 1977, 123-4.

16. Ibid., 124-7.

17. F.C. Bewes, *Kikuyu Conflict*, London, The Highway Press, 1953, 52-8.

18. Anderson, 129-130.

19. Dorothy Smoker, 'Heshbon Mwangi Prays for His Attackers', in Paul M. Lederach, ed., *Story Collection, The Foundation Series*, Scottdale, Mennonite Publishing House, 1978, 337-9.

20. Harold Adeney, *Only One Weapon*, London, Rwanda Mission, C.M.S., 1963, 13.

21. J.C. Wenger, *The Way of Peace*, Scottdale, Herald Press, 1973, 40-1.

22. Anderson, op.cit., 128-32.

23. Ibid., 132-4.

24. Adeney, op. cit., 13.

25. Ibid., 35.

26. Ibid., 37.

27. Ibid., 29.
28. Ibid., 34.
29. Ibid., 47.
30. Bishop Festo Kivengere, *I Love Idi Amin*, Old Tappan, Jersey,
    Fleming H. Revell Co., 1977, 20-21.
31. Letter to His Excellency Al-Hajji Field Marshall Dr. Amin Dada from the
    Church of Uganda, Rwanda, Burundi and Boga-Zaire, 10 February 1977.
32. Ibid,
33. Ibid, 2,3.
34. Kivengere, op. cit., 49,50.
35. Ibid., 55-57.
36. Anderson, op. cit., 127.
37. Martin, op. cit., 102-3, 110-11, 149-52
38. Ibid., 100-13
39. Cecil Eprile, *War and Peace in the Sudan 1955-1972*,
    London, David and Charles 1974, 13-102.
40. Norman Hart, ed., *The Hard Road to Peace,*
    A Report to the Churches of Africa on their part in the Reconciliation in
    the Sudan and an Appeal, Nairobi, All Africa Conference of Churches,
    1972, 5-10.
41. Ibid., 14-17
42. Ibid., 25-26
43. Norman E Thomas, ed., *Rise up and Walk, Bishop Abel Jendekai*
    Muzorewa, An Autobiography, London, Sphere Books Ltd., 1979, 181-7.
44. Canon Burgess Carr, 'The Engagement of Lusaka',
    in Assembly Secretariat, All Africa Conference of Churches,
    The Struggle Continues, Official Report of the Third Assembly,
    All Africa Conference of Churches, Lusaka— Zambia, 12-24.
45. Ibid., 78
46. Kenneth D. Kaunda, 'The Challenge of our Stewardship in Africa', in *The Struggle*
    Continues, et al., 67.
47. Ibid., 67
48 The Struggle Continues, et al., 51
49. Thomas, 174-81
50. *Facing New Challenges, The Message of PACLA, December 9-19, 1972*,
    Nairobi, Kisumu, Kenya, Evangel Publishing House, 1978

153

51. Donald R. Jacobs, 'South African Assembly Convenes',
    Salunga, E.M.B.M.C. Archives,1979, 3.
52. John Foster, *Church History: the First Advance A.D. 29-500*, London,
    SPCK, 1972,75-76.

Chapter VI

CONCLUSION

HISTORICAL-THEOLOGICAL REFLECTIONS ON PEACE

Jesus Christ could not carry his cross. He had not slept the night before. For at least twelve hours he had been shuttled from one part of Jerusalem to another as the travesty of a trial unfolded before the high priest, the king, and the governor. He had been severely beaten with the metal-tipped thongs of Roman justice. The soldiers had pushed a crown of thorns on his head, slapped and mocked him, and spat on his face. The judgment had been proclaimed: He was to be crucified. But he could not carry his cross. His disciples should have been there to step forward and help; but they were not there. In fact Peter, one of Jesus' closest disciples, had denied him three times that very day. The terrified disciples had melted into anonymity. Jesus had no one to help him carry his wooden cross up the gentle rise outside the Jerusalem wall to Golgotha. Who would carry that cross?

The soldiers looked around, perhaps embarrassed that they had beaten their prisoner to such an extent that he was incapable of carrying the cross, saw Simon coming in from the fields and forced him to carry the cross. He was from Cyrene in Libya, North Africa. We do not know why they had to force him. Possibly Simon realized the injustice of the trial and did not want to identify himself with the horror of crucifixion. Nevertheless, by participating in that moment of ignominy, Simon from Libya in Africa helped Jesus with his burden.

Early African Participation in the Cross

Simon's helpfulness reminds us that about thirty-three years earlier Africa herself had opened her arms in compassion and helped Jesus when Joseph and Mary fled with him into Egypt to escape Herod's fury. Africa gave the refugee, Jesus, a home. Both in infancy and death, Africa was present to help, to identify with the pain of rejection

155

and misunderstanding, to participate in the suffering of Christ.

Simon of Cyrene is a symbol of identification with the humiliation and the victory of the cross of Christ. He is a sign of the urgent need for the Church to identify with the cross of Christ. Like Simon, the Church is often 'compelled' by circumstances beyond its control to identify with Christ in his suffering. This is the world-wide experience of the Church; it is also the calling and the mission of the Church in Africa. Millions of Christians have been called and even compelled to follow Simon's example.

This study has focused especially on the modern African participation in the redemptive suffering of Christ. But it is not only in the modern period that the Church in Africa has carried the cross. During the first three centuries of the Christian era it was North African and Egyptian Christians who bore much of the brunt of Roman persecution of Christians. For the early Church of North Africa, martyrdom was the expected consequence of Christian discipleship.

Christian martyrdom in northern Africa during the early centuries of the Christian era was for freedom in Christ. The first written fragment available concerning the North Africa Church is the account of the Scillitan martyrs. They were residents of Numidia, in the hinterland of Carthage. They were condemned to death because they believed that there is no Lord except Christ. These twelve Numidian martyrs died for freedom. They believed that no imperial power had the ultimate authority over their lives. Because Jesus is Lord, they were free people; they had experienced the freedom to die with joy rather than bow to imperial and dehumanizing powers. For these Christian men and women identification with the cross was a witness unto death that, because of Jesus, the person is free.

For the early African martyrs death was the ultimate witness that no imperial power, no man-made Baal, no Caesar whatsoever, dare have the ultimate authority over the person. Only Jesus is Lord. An ancient fragment records the following scene at the trial of an African Christian, Pionius:

Judge:	Will you sacrifice to the genius of the emperor?
Pionius:	No.
Judge:	What is your religion?
Pionius:	The religion of God the Father who made all things.
Judge:	We all worship gods—heaven, the gods in heaven, Zeus the king of the gods.
Pionius:	Silence.
	The warders then tortured him by stretching his body with rope.
The warders:	Now sacrifice.
Pionius:	No.
	The warders then tore his flesh with the iron claw.
The warders:	Change your mind. What madness is this?
Pionius:	Not madness, it is the fear of the living God.
Proconsul:	Why are you so determined upon death?
Pionius:	Not upon death, upon life.[1]

Not death, but life! Imperial Rome was a death system. Tertullian, the great North African lawyer and churchman, decried the injustice of the Roman system with stinging sarcasm and challenged Rome to affirm the dignity and freedom of the human being. Yet even as he wrote, he was aware that his calls for justice could engulf him in the fires of martyrdom. Nevertheless he persisted, for he was confident that in the suffering of the cross there is victory. 'The blood of martyrs is the seed of the Church,' he said. [2]

Tertullian and other early fathers of the Church in North Africa and Egypt believed that the Christian is called to 'share in the suffering of Christ'. (Philippians 3:10.) In fact, there is substantial evidence that the early Church in Africa and elsewhere extended its commitment to the way of the cross right into the question of military service on behalf of the state. Some comments from the early Church fathers in Africa are instructive:

Clement of Alexandria (150-215 A.D.). 'We are being educated, not in war, but in peace. We, the peaceful race, are more temperate than the warlike races.'[3] The Church fathers referred to Christians as the 'new race' because they came from every race and were united in love.

Tertullian of North Africa (160-220 A.D.) 'No dress is lawful among us which is assigned to an unlawful action.'[4] He believed that even the wearing of a military uniform was sub-Christian. In fact, Tertullian demanded that soldiers serving in the army who were converted to Christ should resign their position, even if their resignation meant persecution or death.

Cyprian of Carthage (d 258) 'Enemies are to be loved.'[5] He elaborates that homicide is considered evil when it is done individually, but when the crime is committed in an organized manner by nations and armies, it is considered right by the world. This the Christian cannot accept. War is homicidal savagery. Christians forgive rather than participate in killing.

Origen of Alexandria (185-254). 'For we no longer take up sword against nation nor do we learn war any more, having become children of peace, for the sake of Jesus who is our leader.'[6] He says that the Christian calling is to pray to defeat the demons which stir up war. 'And none fight better for the king than we do. We do not indeed fight under him, although he require it; but we fight on his behalf, forming a special army— an army of piety—by offering our prayers to God.'[7]

The story of a North African youth, Maximilian, reveals that these statements by the Church fathers were not hypothetical. Probably most lay Christians did refuse to serve in the army. Maximilian was one of them. In the year 295 A.D., when he was 21 years old, he was conscripted into the Roman army. He refused to serve.

The military commander demanded: 'Wear the military uniform or we will kill you.'

Maximilian replied, 'I cannot become a soldier because I am a Christian. I cannot do evil.'[8]

He was condemned and executed.

The belief of the early Christians that it was wrong for a Christian to participate in war was so pervasive that Origen felt it was necessary to defend his views on Christian pacifism to the public. Probably one factor contributing to early Christian pacificism was the abhorrence of the sacrificial oaths which all soldiers had to take when entering the army. But this is not the only reason. It is significant that this reason is hardly mentioned by the Church fathers. Their pacifism was anchored in their perceptions of the cross and the nature of the new community.

The Constantinization of the Church

During the fourth century the Church rapidly lost its earlier pacifist perceptions. During Constantine's reign the erosion of early Christian pacifism was swift. How could a Church remain opposed to military duty when the emperor was encouraging the mass baptism of soldiers? Traditional Christian opposition to military service was swiftly swept away as the tidal wave of Constantinization engulfed Christian communities throughout the Roman Empire, including most of the African Church.

That fact is disturbing enough. Of even greater perplexity is the fact that the Church soon began to use the instruments of violence to perpetuate its own interests.

One is saddened and perplexed that the great Augustine of North Africa condoned using imperial armies to forcefully Catholicize the Donatist Church. Even more devastating to the later history of western Christianity is the theological justification which Augustine developed for his anti-Donatist manoeuvers. He believed that whereas all people outside the mother Church are damned, it is part of Christian compassion to compel the lost to come in. Although the Church and state have different functions, the Church is ascendant over the state for it is the sign of the Kingdom of God among people, and therefore it has the right to ask the state to use the instruments of political power and compulsion to establish churchly goals.

The logical outcome of Augustine's theology was forceful military installation of 'Caesar' bishops in Egypt following the popular Coptic rejection of some of the decisions of the Council of Chalcedon. By the fifth century the Constantinization of African Christianity had taken it far afield from Tertullian's theology of martyrdom. Triumphalism had replaced redemptive suffering.

159

A theology of triumphalism is hardly different from that of Islam. In both systems there is no room for a Simon of Cyrene, no need to carry the cross, no need to suffer redemptively. The spread of Islam across north Africa during the seventh century is sobering to all who love the Church. The gradual surrender of the Church to Islamic forms of triumphalistic theology created an eight century erosion of the Christian community. Finally that presence vanished from the land of Augustine. That early African Church is still present only in diminishing numbers in the Nile Valley and Ethiopia.

The Way of the Cross in Western Christianity
Augustinian theology has greatly influenced Western theology in such concepts as the 'just war' which is part of western Christian vocabulary. Selective violence has become an acceptable Christian vocation. In the European experience, Augustinian theology was good political wisdom, because under Constantine's guidance the Church and state became almost cozily synonymous. In that situation redemptive suffering did not make much sense. As a result the place of the cross in human relations has been submerged.

In western Christianity, the power of the cross to create 'a new race' deeply concerned with peace, love, justice and communal harmony has largely been replaced by the emphasis on the cross as a means to *personal* salvation, yet both aspects are irrevocably bound together in the New Testament. Through the cross and the resurrection we receive both forgiveness and a call to a new way of life. (Ephesians 2: 1-8.) This has been side-tracked in western theology and much effort has gone into studying how efficacious grace is and the means of it. Can one receive grace outside the Church? What kind of priesthood effectuates grace? How do sacraments communicate grace? These were the issues, incipient even in the pre-Constantinian era, but dominating much of the Christian theology after Constantine. Although these are important questions, it is equally important for the Church to consider the meaning of the cross in human relations. The meaning of discipleship was largely ignored.

The Cross Reaffirmed

Nevertheless, some Christians have always attempted to live the way of the cross. Within the medieval monastic orders one detects a persistent desire to recapture the suffering-servant motif of New Testament theology. In the self-denial of the monks and nuns a ministry of reconciliation within the wider society is evident. Yet the monastic movement in itself is also a form of retreat, an admission that the pain of the cross in the real world is acute; the cross is lived most effectively in isolation rather than through involvement.

Probably the most persistent vision of the way of the cross in Christian relationships was maintained in some of the eastern churches, which have been suffering minorities for most of their history. Some of these ancient Churches have always been minority communities. For some the rise of Islam in the seventh century nearly overwhelmed, and sometimes continues to threaten, those which survived. Because of their long-drawn suffering, a triumphalistic theology is alien to them. Ministry and witness in suffering, as well as an admission of weakness as a pre-condition to salvation are at the centre of their perceptions of the Gospel.

In the western Church, also, there are some examples of practical cross-bearing which goes beyond an acceptance of suffering in retreat of the monastic movement. There are noteworthy examples of attempts to recover the New Testament commitment to the way of the cross. During the twelfth and thirteenth centuries, the Waldenses shook Europe's secure theological foundations with a heroic commitment to the way of the cross in all of life. Sadly they were persecuted into obscurity.

The sixteenth centuty Anabaptists also energetically attempted to recover a theology of obedient discipleship. Like the North African martyrs, they died by the thousands rather than bow to the church-state system. Their insistence on adult baptism profoundly challenged the church-state system; it was a proclamation of human rights, a manifesto that a human being created in the image of God cannot be forced into faith, a humble insistence that grace is not mediated sacramentally but is experienced in suffering obedience to the One who calls: 'Follow me'. They believed that the essence of the Church is the redeemed community living in obedience. They rediscovered Jesus' affirmation, 'where two or three are gathered in my name, there am I in the midst of them'. (Matthew 18:20.) In their suffering, these Anabaptists did gradually transform the horizon of European and western Church life.

We could mention other examples of revival within the western Church, of commitment to the way of the cross. But the main stream of western theology has never affirmed the normalcy of the cross in Christian human relations. As a result the core of all the New Testament ethics is relegated to irrelevancy, and the Church tends to become a cultural appendage to the state rather than a source in which life is transformed through redemption. This aspect of the western Church is most evident in times of war. The Church rarely attempts to become a reconciler; on the contrary the respective national Christian communities become quite convinced that their side is 'just' and hence bless the war effort of their respective nations. Because the Church is unwilling to identify with the way of the cross in human relations, it also betrays its mission as a leaven and a reconciler in human affairs. The walls which divide people are unchallenged because the Church does not identify with the cross which removes walls.

Today there is a new spirit blowing. Many Christian communities world-wide are taking at least a tentative look into New Testament ethics and are asking new questions about the nature of the Kingdom of God and its relevance to life today. The ferment is noticeable in South America. Theologians such as Gustavo Gutierrez, Paulo Freire, or Orlando Costas have rediscovered Christ's identification with the poor and the oppressed. Yet some of the contemporary South American theologies are tempted into a Marxist dialectic or a European rationalism. Nevertheless, a cry of concern is being raised from South America urging for renewed commitment to the suffering of the cross, especially through identification with the poor.

An African Contribution

This book has been about the African contribution to contemporary understanding of the Kingdom. We have seen that the African perception of God, the person and community is pre-eminently concerned about wholeness of life and harmony in relationships. The Gospel of Jesus Christ enriches that perception; it revolutionizes it too, but always in the context of wholeness in the community. This insight cannot be 'proven'; it needs to be lived. In most African Christian thinking truth is relational; good human relations are truth. God in this context is the truth because He creates harmony. Western man will likely say, God is truth because He is the logical first cause. Speculative truth is not central to the African philosophical heritage. The ground swell of African perceptions of the truth is harmony.

We have seen that the breakdown of harmony is evil, requiring sacrificial suffering to restore harmony. This wisdom has led many Christians in Africa to perceive of the cross life as the way to recreating broken harmony. Repeatedly across the African continent there is a hesitancy to accept interpretations of the cross as only a device for a juridical or sacramental atonement. For many African Christians the cross is more than the means through which God bestows free grace. It is grace indeed, but it can only be achieved at the cost of suffering with the One through whom we experience grace. By suffering at the cross with Jesus we are healed, but our healing can only be complete if harmony is restored in the community, the path to reconciliation, peace and healing.

I believe that one of the greatest contributions of the Church in Africa to the worldwide Christian community today is a deep understanding of redemptive suffering, a witnessing of a Church involved in a ministry of reconciliation, witnessing a new humanity being truly born, a community which transcends the divisions arising out of our sinfulness. Christ crucified and risen stands at the centre of that recreative act of grace. The body of Christ, the Church, becomes a redeemed community of reconciliation by sharing with Christ in his sufferings.

JUSTICE, RECONCILIATION AND PEACE

REFERENCES

1. John Foster, *Church History; The First Advance A.D. 29-500,* London, S.P.C.K., 1972, 75-76.
2. W.H.C. Frend, *The Early Church,* London, Hodder & Stoughton, 1971, 93.
3. C. John Cadoux, *The Early Christian Attitude to War,* London, Headley Brothers, 1919,64.
4. Ibid., 109.
5. Ibid., 81.
6. Robert; and Donaldson, Eds., *The Ante-Nicene Fathers Vol IV,* Buffalo, CLPC, 1885,558
7. Ibid., 668.
8. J.C. Wenger, *The Way of Peace,* Scottdale, Herald Press, 1977, 16.

EPILOGUE

There are countless examples of Christians in reconciliation ministry across Africa. Only a few examples are described in this book. We conclude this chapter with an incident which occurred in the Congo (now Zaire) during the inter-ethnic disturbances which erupted periodically from 1960 to 1965. I mention this incident because it not only illustrates African Christian commitment to reconciliation, but also indicates the manner in which the traditional African heritage often contributes to the perception of the Gospel as being the Good News of reconciliation.

At the dawn of political independence for Zaire in 1960, ethnic rivalries began to destroy the hopes for national unity. One of the tension areas was Charlesville in South Kasai not far south of Luluabourg (Katanga). Charlesville was a church centre where both Baluba and Lulua ethnic societies intermingled. The Church had welded these two groups together into a community of reconciliation. Yet sadly, with the imminent coming of independence, relationships between the two communities in the village of Charlesville and the surrounding hinterland quickly broke down. Violence in the countryside fed animosity in the village. In the midst of the storm the Christian community tried to stand firmly united.

Unity for the Christians was extremely difficult to sustain when kinsmen were being killed in the inter-ethnic violence. Which is stronger, kinship ties or unity in Christ? That was the awesome question for the Christians. Does the new covenant in Christ transcend family loyalty? Many of the Christians continued to live in reconciliation, insisting that in Christ they had become part of the new tribe, the people of Jesus who submit only to the authority of Chief Jesus. That position was terribly difficult to maintain. It demanded radical and continual forgiveness of those enemies who were killing kinsmen.[1]

Finally the war in the countryside was joined in the town of Charlesville itself. It was the last Sunday in May, 1960. Lulua and Baluba young men in the town took to arms and prepared for battle. The armed men stood on opposing sides facing one another. Most

165

of the Christians were also caught in the confrontation. Pitched battle seemed inevitable. The Church leaders were alerted to the impending calamity, and several of the ministers hastened to the battle zone.

The ministers first moved out into the no man's land between the two opposing battle lines. The warriors cried out in fury, 'What are you preachers doing here? Step to one side. Get out. Stop getting yourselves mixed up in our affairs. We're having it out today.'[2]

One of the ministers began to speak. 'The moment a drop of human blood is shed, what will happen? People created by a God of love do not resolve their problems by butchering each other. They solve their problems by using their minds . .. we are the people of God.'[3]

He continued by pointing out that the very ground on which they stood belonged to God. 'It is hallowed ground. Human blood will not be shed here. Not a single drop.'[4]

Finally that small cluster of Church leaders, standing alone in the breach between the two armies, were able to persuade the combatants to accept a peace parley in which the most respected chiefs from each side would discuss the issues and arrange reconciliation. The elders commanded the warriors to return to their homes; the chiefs would negotiate reconciliation; arrows and spears would help nothing.

After a struggle to get the enemies to go home, the Rev. Kuamba finally persuaded the combatants to negotiate reconciliation rather than fight. Holding his Bible for all to see, he stood between the armies and cried out, 'My friends... my kinsmen. Why are you rushing into the direction of fighting rapidly like this? Take your thinking out of the path of war. Don't you fear the warnings of our ancestors about shedding human blood? Fighting will destroy everything. It will divide us perpetually. We are Christians. There is another way to resolve our differences.'[5]

Paul, the apostolic Church planter, wrote to one of the congregations he had founded, a congregation which was in similar circumstances as described above:

EPILOGUE

But now in Christ Jesus you who once were far away have been brought near through the blood of Christ. For he himself is our peace, who has made the two one and has destroyed the barrier, the dividing wall of hostility, by abolishing in his flesh the law with its commandments and regulations. His purpose was to create in himself one new man out of the two, thus making peace and in this one body to reconcile both of them to God through the cross, by which he put to death their hostility. He came and preached peace to you who were far away and peace to those who were near. For through him we both have access to the Father by one Spirit. Consequently you are no longer foreigners and aliens, but fellow citizens with God's people and members of God's household.

(Ephesians 2:13-19)

JUSTICE, RECONCILIATION AND PEACE

REFERENCES

Levi O. Keidel, *War To Be One*, Grand Rapids, Zondervan, 1977, 111-18.
Ibid., 121.
Ibid.
Ibid.
Ibid., 122.

APPENDIX

FORCE AND POWER
by Bishop Festo Kivengere

'Black Power,' 'Chicano Power.' 'student power' and 'power blocs' are a few of the power words we hear these days. This era may be referred to as the 'decade in search of power'.

However, in most of the claimed 'powers,' there is an uncomfortable awareness, in varying degrees, of helplessness. This latent, unadmitted feeling of inability to cope keeps erupting in many ways.

In the desperate effort to bring situations under a sort of transitory control, 'powers' use force as their weapon, either to suppress or to eliminate the threat. So, under pressure, they all tend to become tyrannous.

When 'power' uses force, it confesses its inability to cope with that which threatens it. In using force, it admits that it cannot change the situation, and so turns to methods of elimination.

A thief, scared to death by an unexpected intruder, turns to his gun in despair. He has no power to change him, so he turns to the cheap method of shooting him.

A politically powerful racial or tribal minority becomes scared of the resentments of the majority it has exploited and, in despair of ever making them friends, turns to the weapons of suppression and elimination.

The oppressed, finding that they are utterly unable to change their oppressors, often apply the same weapons of despair—terrorism and destruction, burnings, threats, bitterness and hatred. All these have one confession, not of power, but of despair.

When power fails to create, then it has no right to be called 'power'. It is force in despair. Force is blind, and usually destructive.

Saul of Tarsus, whom we know as Paul, thought he had power. He had authority from the hierarchy, the power-structure of Judaism. He was going to see that the Christians were erased from the face of Palestine. He couldn't stand them.

In a sense, however, he was very weak—that is why he used force. If he had been powerful, instead of eliminating the Christians, he would have had the ability to change them.

Then one day the force of Saul met the power of Christ (Acts 9:1-19.) Saul was on his way to destroy, Christ was on His way to create, to give life, not to take life away. Jesus met His enemy and simply asked him,

'Why are you persecuting Me, a crucified Christ?'

How can a crucified Christ be the power of God, as Paul said afterwards in 1 Corinthians 1:23, 24. Can one who, on the cross, could not even drive the flies away from His face be the Power of God, changing Saul into Paul?

But that is where power lies. The cross is where the action is. For on the cross we are not looking at a tragic victim of circumstances, but on a willing Sufferer, with love so powerful that it is stronger than death.

There was Jesus, dying on the cross, men driving nails into His hands to kill Him, and He prays, 'Father, forgive these men, they don't understand!' That is power meeting the world of hatred and changing it into love.

There are people who talk as if a person who forgives his enemies has no guts. Spiritual guts are the kind that can forgive an enemy and change him.

So far as I am concerned, the only real power I know is the power of Christ, and Him on the cross. Through His sacrificial love, power is released to meet broken men and women, broken by hatred, fear, suspicion, tyranny and oppression, and change them into friends, brothers and sisters.

Ours is a society that takes up guns and knives and begins to throw them at its members. It is a society in despair, full of fear, disintegrated and weak.

Jesus is able to make a new life for a man who is the victim of drugs or drunkenness, a victim of his desires, or of hatred and fear, who seems hopeless to the rest of the world.

Jesus does this, not with a big stick, hitting him on the head —that would destroy him; not with hatred – that would embitter him; not with tyranny—that would freeze him, but with love. His is the eternal, mighty love which takes a person, puts the pieces together, and out of nothing gives you a new human being.

I may be permitted to give a little testimony of what that power did for me on the day when I met the Lord. I began immediately to tell others the miracle of God's liberating love. Then God began to send me through the fields to people to ask for forgiveness and to tell them that my hang-ups about them had now been completely removed.

I remember one day when I went fifty miles on a bicycle to a white man whom I had hated and whom I had frozen because I, too, had been frozen. There I stood in his house, telling what Christ had done for me, and that I was free and saw him now as my brother! That man stood there, English as he was, amazed. I did not use a stick or a spear, but by the time I left, we were brothers.

I can also tell how our brothers faced the Mau Mau in Kenya. Hundreds of them were caught in that terrible confusion of hatred. Now hatred usually has a good reason, and there was a good reason for the Kikuyu to hate the white people who had taken away their land, and therefore had robbed them.

But there were men in Kenya who had fallen in love with Christ, who is the Power of God. They had been released from the weakness of hatred, and they refused to hate. Because they refused to hate, their fellow tribesmen regarded them as traitors, 'whites in black skin'. And the whites, who expected them to fight their Mau Mau brothers, also condemned them as 'Mau Mau in disguise', because these Christians refused to take guns.

They said, 'Our gun is love. We love the Mau Mau and we love the white men. We feel that the white men, in robbing us of our land, were sick. They need medicine, and the medicine is the love of Christ. We feel that the Mau Mau, in getting out their knives to cut everybody, are sick to despair, and we are going to love them into liberty.'

They suffered, and some of them died. Some were hacked to pieces, but they died loving and witnessing. Out of their suffering testimony, men were released. Men who had been terrorists were converted to Jesus Christ. Many, also, of the sophisticated white settlers were challenged, and some of them were converted. I heard the testimony of some. They were struck, not with a knife, but with the love of Christ through these black Christians who truly had power, power to love, to create and restore.

I see the love of Jesus Christ upon the cross. And I can see the black and the white, the brown and the red, each with his respective colour, all gathered together, bringing all their angers toward each other and putting them down at the foot of the cross. At the feet of Him who loved His enemies, they lay down their weapons, their hatred, resentment, bitterness and cutting remarks. One looks the other in the face, white as he is, black as he is, and discovers Jesus' love there.

Then, in that atmosphere of Christ's love, men are healed, restored, recreated. And out of the confusion, God produces a new community, men and women who see each other as brothers and sisters because Jesus loves them.

BIBLIOGRAPHY

Achebe,Chinua, *Arrow of God,* London, Heinemann., 1975.

Adeney, Harold, *Only One Weapon,* London, Rwanda Mission, CMS 1963.

Adeyemo, Tokunboh, *Salvation in African Tradition,* Nairobi, Evangel Publishing House, 1979.

African Christian Peace Conference, *Speeches and Documents,* West Africa, 1977.

Ahanotu, Austin Metu Mara, Editor, *Religion, State and Society in contemporary Africa,* New York, Peter Lang, 1987.

Anderson, W.B. *The Church in East Africa,* 1840-1974, Dodoma, Central Tanganyika Press, 1977.

Barrett, David B., *African Initiatives in Religion,* Nairobi, East African Publishing House, 1971.

Barrett, David B., *Schism and Renewal in Africa; An Analysis of Six Thousand Contemporary Religious Movements,* Nairobi, Oxford University Press, 1968.

Bediako, Kwame, *Christianity in Africa,* Maryknoll, New York, Orbis, 1995.

Bewes, T.F.C., *Kikuyu Conflict,* London, The Highway Press, 1953.

Bosch, David J., *A Spirituality of the Road,* Scottdale, Herald Press, 1979.

Bright, John, *The Kingdom of God,* Nashville, Abingdon, 1953.

Buhlmann, Walbert, *The Coming of the The Third Church,* New York, Orbis, 1977.

Cadoux, C.John, *The Early Christian Attitudes to War,* London, Headley Brothers, 1919.

Cassidy, Virlinden, *Facing the New Challenges, the Messages of PACLA,* Kisumu, Evangel Publishing House, 1978.

Chureh J.E., *Quest for The Highest,* Exeter, Paternoster Press, 1982.

Dickson, Kwesi and Ellingworth, Paul, *Biblical Revelation and African Beliefs,* New York, Orbis Books, 1969.

Donovan, Vincent J., *Christianity Rediscovered, An Epistle from the Maasai,* Notre Dame, Fides, Claretian, 1978.

Ela, Jean-Marc, *My Faith as an African*, Maryknoll, New York, Orbis 1990.

Eprile, Cecil, *War and Peace in the Sudan*, 1955-1972, David and Charles, 1974.

Foster, John, *Church History: The First Advance A.D. 29-500*, London, S.P.C.K. 1972.

Frend, W.H.C., *The Early Church*, London, Hodder & Stoughton, 1971.

Gibson, Richard, *African Liberation Movements*, London, Oxford University Press,1972.

Gikoyo, Gucu G., *We Fought for Freedom*, Nairobi, East African Publishing House, 1979.

Girald Rone, *Violence and the Sacred*, London, The John Hopkins University Press, 1977.

Githige, Renison Muchiri, 'The Religious Factor in Mau Mau with Particular Reference to Mau Mau Oaths,' M.A Thesis, Nairobi, University of Nairobi, 1978.

Glasswell, Mark E., and Fashole-Luke, Edward W., Editors, *New Testament Christianity for Africa and the World, Essays in Honour of Harry Sawyerr*, London,S.P.C.K. 1974.

Idowu, E. Bolaji, *African Traditional Religion: A Definition*, London, SCM Press, 1973.

Idowu, E. Bolaji *Olodumare: God in Yoruba Belief*, London, Longman, 1962.

Jahn, Janheinz, *Muntu: The New African Culture*, New York, Grove Press,Inc., 1961.

Jassy, Marie-France Penin, *Basic Community in the African Churches*, New York, Orbis Books, 1973.

Kato, Byang, *Theological Pitfalls in Africa*, Nairobi, Evangel Publishing House, 1974.

Kaunda, Kenneth, *A Humanist in Africa*, New York, Abingdon Press, 1966.

Kaunda, Kenneth, *Letter to My Children*, London, Longman, 1973.

Kealy, John P., & Shenk, David W., *The Early Church and Africa*, Nairobi, Oxford University Press, 1975.

Keidel, Levi O., *War To Be One*, Michigan, Zondervan Publishing House, 1977.

BIBLIOGRAPHY

Kenyatta, Jomo, *Facing Mount Kenya,* London, Secker and Warburg, 1938, reprinted by Mercury Books, 1961.

Kenyatta, Jomo, *Suffering Without Bitterness*, Nairobi, East African Publishing House, 1968.

Kibicho, Samuel G., *'The Kikuyu Conception of God, His Continuity into the Christian Era and the Question it Raises for the Christian Idea of Revelation,'* unpublished Ph. D. dissertation, Nashville, Vanderbilt University, 1972.

Kivengere, Bishop Festo, *I Love Idi Amin,* New Jersey, Fleming H. Revell Company, 1977.

Knappert, Jan, *Myths and Legends of the Swahili* London, Heinemann, 1970.

Larom, Margaret S., Editor, *Claiming the promise: African Churches speak,* New York, Friendship Press, 1994.

Lederach, Paul M., editor, *Story Collection,* Scottdale, Mennonite Publishing House, 1978.

Luthuli, Albert, *Let My People* Go, New York, McGraw-Hill, 1962.

Mandela, Nelson, *No Easy Walk to Freedom,* London, Heinemann, 1965.

Martin, Marie-Louise, *Kimbangu, An African Prophet and His Church,* Grand Rapids MI, Eerdmans, 1976.

Mbiti, John S., *African Religions and Philosophy,* London, Heinemann, 1971.

Mbiti, John S., *Concepts of God in Africa,* London, S.P.C.K., 1970.

Mbiti, John S., *New Testament Eschatology in an African Background,* London, S.PC.K., 1970.

Mbiti, John S., *Poems of Nature and Faith,* Nairobi, East African Publishing House, 1969.

McVeigh, Malcolm J., *God in Africa: Concepts of God in African Traditional Religion and Christianity,* Hartford, Claude Stark, 1974.

Moore, Basil, *Black Theology,* London, C. Hurst & Company, 1973.

Mugambi, Jesse and Kirima, Nicodemus, *The African Religious Heritage,* Nairobi, Oxford University Press, 1976.

Muzorewa, Bishop Abel T., *Rise Up and Walk,* London, Sphere Books, Ltd., 1979.

Newbigin, J.E. Lesslie, *Honest Religion for Secular Man,* London, S.C.M., 1966.

Nyerere, Julius K., *Freedom and Development,* London, Oxford University Press, 1974.

Oglesby, Enoch H. *Born in Fire,* New York, Pilgrim Press, 1990.

Okullu, Henry, *Church and Politics in East Africa,* Nairobi, Uzima Press, 1974.

Olupona, Jacob K., editor, *African Traditional Religions in Contemporary Society,* (From the Conference, *The Place of African Traditional Religion in Contemporary Africa; Nairobi 1987.* New York, Paragon House, 1991)

Oruka, H. Odera, *Punishment and Terrorism in Africa,* Nairobi, East African Literature Bureau, 1976.

Paris, Peter J., *The Spirituality of African Peoples: The Search for a Common Moral discourse,* Minneapolis; Fortress Press, 1995.

Parratt, John, *Reinventing Christianity; African Theology Today* Grand Rapids, MI, Eerdmans, 1995.

Parrinder, E.G., *African Traditional Religion,* London, Sheldon Press, 1954.

p'Bitek, Okot, *Africa's Cultural Revolution,* Nairobi, Macmillan, 1973.

p' Bitek, Okot, *Religion of the Central Luo,* Nairobi, East African Literature Bureau, 1971.

Pobee, John S., *Toward An African Theology,* Nashville, Abingdon, 1979.

Pritchard, E.E.I. Evans, *Nuer Religion,* London, Oxford University Press, 1956.

Sawyerr, Harry, *God: Ancestor or Creator?* London, Longman, 1970.

Schreiter, Robert J., Editor, *Faces of Jesus in Africa,* Maryknoll, Orbis, 1991.

Senghor, Leopold Sedar, *Nocturnes,* New York, Joseph Okpaku Publishing Company, Inc.,1971.

Shorter, Aylward, *African Christian Spirituality,* London, Geoffrey Chapman, 1978.

Shorter, Aylward, *African Christian Theology,* London, Geoffrey Chapman, 1975.

Shorter, Aylward, *African Culture and the Christian Church*, London, Geoffrey Chapman, 1975.

Shorter, Aylward, *Prayer in the Religious Traditions of Africa*, Nairobi, Oxford University Press, 1975.

Smoker, Dorothy, *Ambushed by Love: God's Triumph in Kenya's Terror*, Fort Washington, P.A., Christian Literature Crusade, 1993.

Snell, Elaine Murray, *Uganda: Fire and Blood*, New Jersey, Logos International, 1977.

Taylor, John B., *Primal World Views*, Ibadan, Daystar Press, 1976.

Taylor, John V., *The Primal Vision*, London S.C.M., 1963.

Tempels, Placide, *Bantu Philosophy*, Paris, Presence Africaine, 1959.

Thiong'o, Ngugi wa, *The River Between*, London, Heinemann,1978.

Thiong'o, Ngugi wa, and Mugo, Micere Githae, *The Trial of Dedan Kimathi*, Nairobi, Heinemann Educational Books, 1976.

Tihagale, Ruti and Itumeleng Mosala, editors, *Hammering swords into plow shares, Essays in Honour of Archbiship Tutu*, Grand Rapids MI, Eerdmans, 1987.

Torres, Sergio and Fabella, Virginia, editors, *The Emergent Gospel*, New York, Orbis, 1976.

Tuma, Tom and Mutibwa, Phares, editors, *A Century of Christianity in Uganda*, 1877-1977, Nairobi, Afropress Limited,1978.

Tutu, Desmond, editor, *An African Prayer Book*, New York, Doubleday, 1995.

Twesigye, Emmanuel K., *Common Ground: Christianity, African Religion and Philosophy*, New York, Peter Lang, 1987.

Van Leeuwen, Arend Theodoor, *Christianity in World History*, New York, Charles Scribner & Sons,1964.

Wai, Dunstan M., editor,*The Southern Sudan: The Problem of National Integration*, Great Britain, St. Ann's Press, 1973.

Wenger, J.C., *The Way of Peace*, Scottdale, Herald Press.

Wilson, Monica, *Religion and the Transformation of Society*, Cambridge University Press, 1971.

Wipper, Audrey, *Rural Rebels*, Nairobi, Oxford University Press, 1977.

Yoder, John H., *ThePolitics of Jesus*, Grand Rapids MI, Eerdmans, 1972.

Printed by Act Print Ltd, Lunga Lunga Road,
P.O. Box 48127, Nairobi.